US MILIT...
VEHICL...
FIELD GUIDE

David Doyle

WORLD WAR II - PRESENT

©2005 KP Books
Published by

kp books
An Imprint of F+W Publications

700 East State Street • Iola, WI 54990-0001
715-445-2214 • 888-457-2873
Our toll-free number to place an order or obtain
a free catalog is (800) 258-0929.

Library of Congress Catalog Number: 2005924826
ISBN: 0-89689-270-0

Designed by Kay Sanders
Edited by Dennis Thornton

Printed in United States of America

Contents

One-Ton Trucks

One-and-One-Quarter Ton Trucks

One-and-One-Half Ton Trucks

Two-and-One-Half Ton Trucks

Four-Ton Trucks

Five-Ton Trucks

Six-Ton Trucks

Contents

5

Section 2 Tracked Vehicles

Contents

Main Battle Tanks

Armored Personnel Carriers

Amphibious Landing Vehicles

Carriers

Self-Propelled Artillery

Half Track Vehicles

High Speed Tractors

Armored Recovery Vehicles

Contents

INTRODUCTION

"You go to war with the Army you have, not the Army you might want or wish to have at a later time."

Though often criticized by pundits, truer words than these, spoken by Secretary of Defense Donald Rumsfeld in December 2004, have not been uttered. This is particularly true in the field of military vehicles.

Each generation of American military vehicles represents the lessons learned, and hence the wishes, from the previous war. Improved flotation, increased cargo capacity, higher speeds and personnel heaters all resulted from the lessons of World War II and were features of the next generation of vehicles–vehicles that were too late for World War II, but appeared on the Korean battlefield.

The fully-enclosed armored personnel carriers so prevalent in Vietnam were not built for that war. Rather, they were the wishes of troops in the Korean War. And so it goes. Each generation of soldiers rides to war on chariots not of their wishes, but those of the generation before.

World War II brought America's manufacturing might to the forefront. Thousands of vehicles from a host of manufacturers were rushed to battlefields around the world. At the same time, however, the diversity of parts in the supply system due to the range of vehicles and manufacturers pointed to the need of standardization.

This was accomplished in the "M-series" vehicles that were introduced in 1949. Electrical components, circuit numbers, instruments, tire sizes and a range of components were standardized. At the same time, both shallow and deep water fording abilities were added, eliminating the need for hours of tedious preparation prior to crossing streams or making amphibious landings. Twenty-four volt electrical systems were standardized, allowing radios to be fitted to any vehicle, rather than just specially prepared vehicles as was the case in World War II.

The vehicles created in this process are only now leaving the military's inventory. In their place is an array of increasingly sophisticated vehicles. The HMMWV, HEMMT, Bradley and Abrams, for example, have been fielded, each designed for better protection of the GI than previously thought possible.

Many of the older vehicles have been offered as surplus, many of them bought by farmers, contractors and loggers–all benefiting from the "go anywhere" characteristics of the former military vehicles. Of the vehicles in collectors' hands today, only a few have gone directly from the military to the enthusiast. Most have passed through one or more intermediate owners, either civilian or municipal. States and cities, as well as other government agencies, benefit from a generous Department of Defense donation program. As a rule, the more intermediate owners the vehicle has had, the more challenging the restoration.

Through the years, the military's surplus program has changed. First, armored vehicles were no longer offered as surplus. Then wheeled vehicles, first the M151 MUTT, then the Gama Goat and GOER, then later the HMMWV, were all declared unsuitable for surplus sales. Retired vehicles of these series were to be destroyed, rather than sold. These policies, coupled with serious restrictions on the importation of military hardware formerly owned by the U.S. government, notably Lend-Lease vehicles, have pushed the prices of preserved vehicles upwards.

VALUE AND RARITY

There are almost infinite variations of vehicles, even of the same model. The pricing shown in this Field Guide represents current market trends for typical examples of each vehicle. Some vehicles are so rarely traded that it is impractical to attempt to establish a market value, either because of scarcity or current military usage.

One major factor in determining value is on vehicle material (OVM) or basic issue items (BIIL). This can range from a jack, lug wrench and a few basic hand tools for an MB Jeep, to a list of hundreds of tools carried on contact maintenance trucks. In some cases, the value of the OVM can exceed the value of the base vehicle. To be considered in the top grade, a vehicle must include all the BIIL equipment required to be considered mission ready by the military.

Rarity is, of course, initially driven by production quantity and also by survivability and accessibility. The rarity of vehicles in this book are rated on a scale of 1 through 5, with 1 being the most common (M-37, for example), and 5 being the scarcest (M-386 rocket launcher, for example).

CONDITION

Not only does condition affect the price of a given vehicle, it also affects its collectibility. Another factor closely related is the quality of restoration.

A preserved vehicle is maintained in a "state of suspended animation." All the flaws, scratches and rust that are present when the vehicle is "discovered" are preserved. While this style of collecting is more popular with vehicle enthusiasts overseas than in this country, it is commonplace in other areas of collecting such as furniture.

The term "restoration" is often ill defined or improperly used in the military vehicle hobby. Oftentimes what some call a restoration is actually a representation, and sadly, sometimes is only a characterization. For a true military vehicle restoration, one must know the history of that particular vehicle. Once known, it is then important to define what time frame the vehicle is to be restored to. This could be as it appeared as it left the factory, or at any subsequent time (June 6, 1944, March 3, 1952, etc.). Because the military is constantly improving, upgrading and modifying its vehicles, the date you wish to return to must be defined. For example, while M35 cargo trucks were used during the Korean conflict, none of them had composite-type taillights at that time. To be restored to factory condition, a vehicle would need to have all the equipment supplied at the factory, but no more. Ambulances, for example, didn't leave the factory outfitted with equipment and medical supplies, nor did Jeeps leave the plant with machine guns and deep water fording pipes installed.

Oftentimes, the difference between restoration and a representation is misunderstood. An example of this could be rebuilding, painting and marking a Jeep to look like one driven on the beach at Normandy, even though the Jeep you own never left North America. While not a true restoration, this type of representation is the most popular with collectors.

Safety-based modifications, such as seat belts and turn signals, tastefully done, are normally overlooked by judges at shows.

Condition

VEHICLE CONDITION SCALE

The vehicles in this book are given a value based on a 1-to-6 condition grading scale:

1=Excellent: Restored to maximum professional standards, or a near-perfect original.

2=Fine: Well-restored, or a combination of superior restoration and excellent original parts.

3=Very Good: Complete and operable original or older restoration, or a very good amateur restoration with all presentable and serviceable parts inside and out.

4=Good: Functional or needing only minor work to be functional. Also, a deteriorated restoration or poor amateur restoration.

5=Restorable: Needs complete restoration of body, chassis, and interior. May or may not be running, but is not wrecked, weathered or stripped to the point of being useful only for parts.

6=Parts Vehicle: Deteriorated beyond the point of restoration.

Condition code	6	5	4	3	2	1	Scarcity
Value (dollars)	2,000	5,000	10,000	13,000	17,000	20,000	2

Value/rarity (this information is not included on vehicles still being bought by the Army (Abrams, Bradley, FMTV, etc.)

Section 1 Wheeled Vehicles
Motorcycles

Fran Blake

Condition code	6	5	4	3	2	1	Scarcity
Value (dollars)	2,000	5,000	10,000	13,000	17,000	20,000	5

Wheeled Vehicles

Harley-Davidson WLA

During World War II, both the Allies and the Axis nations used thousands of motorcycles. Although the advent of the Jeep significantly reduced the role of the motorcycle in U.S. military strategy, both Harley-Davidson and Indian produced numerous models of motorcycles for military use.

Harley-Davidson had built motorcycles for the military since World War I, and the famed World War II-era WLA was simply the latest in a long series of government sales. Today, it is the Harley-Davidson WLA that most often comes to mind when the term "Army motorcycle" is heard.

These bikes were based on Harley's civilian model WL, modified with the addition of military items. The 42-WLA is what most collectors are referring to when they say "WLA."

The powerplant, the classic 45 cubic-inch Harley-Davidson 45-degree V-twin, could push the bike to speeds up to 70 mph. The motorcycle featured right side chain drive with three-speed gearbox. Included was such military gear as a scabbard for a Thompson submachine gun on the right side of the front fork, blackout lights on the front and rear, a crankcase skidplate and a substantial luggage rack.

Weight:	513 pounds
Size (LxWxH):	88" x 36.25" x 59"
Range:	124 miles

Doug Mitchel

Condition code	6	5	4	3	2	1	Scarcity
Value (dollars)	1,500	3,000	4,000	8,000	15,000	22,000	5

Harley-Davidson XA

As the Germans waged war in the desert of North Africa, the toll taken by sand and grit was enormous. That, coupled with its experiences in the dust and mud of Russia, convinced the Wehrmacht that shaft drive would be preferable. Both BMW and Zündapp created shaft-drive motorcycles. These developments did not escape the attention of the U.S. War Department, which in turn had both Harley-Davidson and Indian develop similar bikes. Harley-Davidson based its entry, the Model XA, on the BMW design. In 1941, the Quartermaster Corps contracted for 1,000 of the model 42-XA. Not all those built were issued, and the bulk of those that were used were employed only in testing and training functions. Production ceased in 1943.

The 23 horsepower, 45 cubic-inch engine, unlike the classic Harley V-twin design, was used instead of an opposed piston design and featured a carburetor for each cylinder.

While the performance of the XA was adequate, in many people's opinion, it unnecessarily diverted production facilities and introduced more parts into the supply chain.

Weight: 525 pounds
Wheelbase: 59.5
Horsepower: 23

Denise Moss

Condition code	6	5	4	3	2	1	Scarcity
Value (dollars)	3,000	7,000	20,000	29,000	37,000	45,000	4

Harley-Davidson Big Twin

Much larger than either the WLA or the UA, the Harley-Davidson U, used by the Navy, and the UA, used by the Army, were based on a prewar civilian Harley-Davidson. Powered by Harley's 74 cubic-inch flathead engine, the additional power was required because of the sidecar that was installed on these bikes.

The Navy procured some of these sidecar-equipped model U bikes and employed them with the Shore Patrol, among other things.

Initially the Quartermaster ordered 335 of the UA, with a further 504 ordered in 1940. However, this was the extent of the Army orders, making this a rare bike today.

Because these machines were not meant for front line or combat use, they are often mistaken for civilian Big Twins.

A spare tire was on the rear of the sidecar. The sidecar's windshield was hinged, and could be tilted forward to allow the passenger to get in and out.

Weight: 850 pounds
Size (LxWxH): 96" x 69" x 42"
Max Speed: 55 mph

Clark Bennett

Condition code	6	5	4	3	2	1	Scarcity
Value (dollars)	1,700	5,000	8,000	16,000	30,000	38,000	4

Indian 340-B

By the early 1930s, Indian and Harley-Davidson were the only two American producers of motorcycles. Indian had suffered through years of bungling management following the departure of founders George Hendee and Oscar Hedstrom in 1915 and 1913, respectively. However, in 1929, brothers Francis I. and E. Paul DuPont (yes, that DuPont family) bought large amounts of stock in the struggling company and brought in better management.

As world events turned toward war, Indian struggled to regain market share lost during the previous two decades and military interest in motorcycles was renewed. Once war broke out in Europe, the governments of England and France placed orders for motorcycles, and Indian was the beneficiary.

The 74 cubic-inch 340 and 344 Chiefs were big, powerful bikes, considerably larger than the more familiar Harley-Davidson WLA and Indian 640-B.

The additional horsepower and more rugged construction were required to allow the installation of a sidecar without overburdening the chassis, particularly in off-road conditions. The Germans did this on the 45 cubic-inch BMW R75 and KS 750 sidecar bikes by powering the wheel on the sidecar as well as the rear wheel of the bike. Indian addressed this problem in the typical American fashion: it installed a bigger engine.

Prior to the U.S. Army adopting the "Jeep" as the standard light reconnaissance, courier and utility vehicle, large numbers of the Indian Chief, or 340-B, powered by a 74 cubic-inch engine were ordered. In 1944, the government of Australia ordered in quantity a slightly updated model of the Chief, the 344.

Weight:	550 pounds
Wheelbase:	62"
Horsepower:	40
Max Speed:	75 mph

Condition code	6	5	4	3	2	1	Scarcity
Value (dollars)	1,000	2,000	3,000	6,000	10,000	16,000	3

Robin Markey

Indian 741-B

The model produced in greatest numbers for the war effort, the 741, was created for the British. In April 1941, Col. J.H. Smith of the British Purchasing Commission expressed the desire of the Empire to purchase motorbikes lighter in weight and more fuel-efficient than the then-current 45 cubic-inch Indians and Harley-Davidsons. It was decided to create a new machine with a 30.50 cubic-inch engine and use as many parts as possible from the model 640 then in production. Series production of the 741 began in December 1941, even before the testing was completed and, though the war clouds burst into storm for the nation, the future looked bright for Indian.

During the design process of the 741, the size of the engine was changed again, to 30.07 cubic inches, but the 30-50 moniker stuck. With a three-speed transmission and conventional chain drive, the bike could attain 70 mph.

An early complaint from the British about the tires resulted in two-ply tires being installed on vehicles bound for England, with four-ply tires being used on bikes destined for Australia. Four-ply tires were installed on all late production 741s.

At $2,062,000, the first of the Lend-Lease contracts dwarfed the earlier foreign military sales orders, but it was to be by no means the largest.

Legend has it that many of the 5,000 Indians France ordered in October 1939 were lost before delivery when the SS Hanseatic Star was torpedoed. But no documentation has surfaced to support that a ship of this name existed at that time, much less that it took thousands of Indians to an early, watery grave.

◆

Weight:	513 pounds
Size (LxWxH):	88" x 34" x 40"
Horsepower:	15
Max Speed:	65 mph

◆

John Lacko

Condition code	6	5	4	3	2	1	Scarcity
Value (dollars)	1,200	2,500	5,000	11,000	15,000	22,000	5

Indian 841

This shaft-drive motorcycle was created at the behest of the U.S. Army, and was intended to duplicate the success of BMW's shaft drive motorcycles in the desert. The dust, grit and sand of North Africa wore heavily on conventional chain drives, whose oil attracted these contaminants and held them in place, wearing the chain. In 1941, the U.S. Army ordered 1,000 shaft-drive bikes each from both Indian and Harley-Davidson. However, Indian records indicate that a handful more than the originally contracted 1,000 bikes were produced.

Indian designed a new engine for its shaft-drive bike. Based on the Scout's 45 cubic-inch powerplant, but with the angle of the block spread from 45 degrees to 90 degrees, it was mounted sideways in the frame. Its protruding cylinder heads gave the bike a distinctive appearance. A newly designed four-speed foot-shift gearbox was mounted and coupled to a driveshaft. The 841's tubular, plunger-suspended frame and final drive units were much like the BMW bikes that so ably served the German army in horrible conditions.

A few were used in testing, a few more were used in training, evidently none were used in combat, and most of the unused bikes were sold on the surplus market at the end of the war.

Indian's 841 shaft-drive model, a personal favorite of company President E. Paul DuPont, held great promise for postwar development in the civilian marketplace. However, when the DuPonts sold their stock and left Indian, the dream of civilian Indian shaft drives left too.

◆

Weight:	550 pounds
Cubic Inch	45
Displacement:	
Max Speed:	75 mph

◆

Quarter-Ton Trucks

Condition code	6	5	4	3	2	1	Scarcity
Value (dollars)	3,500	10,000	16,000	23,500	30,000	36,000	5

Bantam BRC-40 Reconnaissance Car

The vehicle that is now known world wide as the Jeep was born in Butler, Pa., in the shops of the American Bantam Car Co. Beyond that, the story gets a bit fuzzy. There are almost as many explanations of the origin of the term "Jeep" as there were Jeeps built. Karl Probst is widely credited with the design of the Jeep, but Probst was a latecomer in the process. Bantam's engineering team included Harold Crist, Ralph Turner and Chet Hemphling. (Crist and Hemphling later being instrumental in Mid-America Research Corp.'s development of the M422 Mighty-Mite.)

After a few minor design changes, the design was approved and work began on 69 pre-production units. Eight of these were four-wheel steer models and all were completed by Dec. 17, 1940. These original Bantams had a rounded grille and rounded fenders, and were designated Bantam Model 60.

The second batch of Bantams was an order for 1,500 vehicles, which were constructed from March 10 through July 2, 1941. These and succeeding units built by Bantam were known as BRC-40s. Before production commenced on these vehicles, the design was changed to incorporate a flat hood and grille, and a two-piece windshield. According to testimony of Francis Fenn, Bantam president, before the Truman committee, in addition to the eight four-wheel-steer Model 60s, there were 50 four-wheel-steer BRC-40s built. Bantam's third and last order for reconnaissance cars was for only 1,175 units, and work was completed on them in December 1941. Bantam produced torpedoes for the Royal Navy, and thousands of 1/4-ton T-3 trailers for use behind Jeeps, but after December 1941 its days of producing the 1/4-ton reconnaissance vehicle were done.

The first Bantam Reconnaissance Car was constructed in just 47 days and, two days later, Crist drove it to Camp Holabird, Baltimore. All the Bantams were powered by the 48 horsepower Continental Y-4112 six-cylinder engine.

Weight:	2,600 pounds
Size (LxWxH):	126" x 54" x 72"
Max Speed:	55 mph
Range:	165 miles

Veteran's Memorial Museum, Huntsville, Ala.

Condition code	6	5	4	3	2	1	Scarcity
Value (dollars)	1,500	2,000	3,500	9,000	16,000	24,000	4

Ford GP

Ford and Willys scrambled to create a vehicle competitive with Bantam's Reconnaissance Car. Ford's entry was the Pygmy. Ford modified one of its standard tractor engines to power the Pygmy, but the "Go-Devil" powering Willys' Quad proved superior.

Ford constructed a second prototype, this time using a body supplied by Philadelphia's Budd Company. This version more closely resembled the Bantam body with its unusually shaped door openings. Only one vehicle of this design was produced and, surprisingly, it survives today.

Fifteen hundred reconnaissance trucks were ordered each from Bantam, Willys and Ford for extended service trials. The Ford vehicle delivered was assigned the Ford product designation GP. Using Ford's standard product codes, G refers to government contract vehicle, P indicating an 80-inch wheelbase reconnaissance car. In addition to the 1,500 vehicles on the initial contract, a further 2,958 units were built on later orders.

Many of the attributes now associated with Jeep were in fact developed by Ford, and introduced with the Pygmy. These included grille-mounted headlights, dog-legged windshield hinges and squared-off hood.

Fifty of these vehicles were experimentally equipped with four-wheel steering. This idea was abandoned as excessively dangerous, as well as adding numerous parts to the supply channel.

◆

Weight: 2,100 pounds
Size (LxWxH): 129" x 62" x 71"
Max speed: 55 mph
Range: 165 miles

◆

Condition code	6	5	4	3	2	1	Scarcity
Value (dollars)	1,500	2,000	3,500	9,000	16,000	24,000	4

Willys MA

The first vehicle built by Willys as part of the Reconnaissance Car competition was the Quad. Despite its strong powerplant, the design itself had some shortcomings. For the 1,500-vehicle trial run, the Quad was redesigned, becoming the MA. The Willys name was embossed in the front of all the MA vehicles. Willys built 1,553 of these vehicles, the bulk of which, like the Bantam BRC-40, were supplied to Russia under Lend-Lease arrangements. Production of the MA ran from June 5, 1941, through Sept. 23, 1941. Today the MA is an extremely difficult vehicle to find in the United States.

The MA featured a flat hood, full-length front fenders with headlamps mounted on them and column shift for the transmission.

Weight: 2,450 pounds

Condition code	6	5	4	3	2	1	Scarcity
Value (dollars)	800	4,500	9,000	12,000	16,000	20,000	1

Willys MB

After 1,500 units each of the Bantam BRC-40, Ford GP and Willys MA had been tried, it was time for the Jeep to go into mass production. Willys was awarded a contract for an improved MA, known as the MB.

The first 20,700 MBs used solid disk wheels, after which combat wheels were used. Like its Willys predecessors, the "Go-Devil" engine powered the MB. This practice was discontinued in July 1942. From March 16, 1941, through Aug. 20, 1945, Willys-Overland bought its bodies from American Central (formerly known as Auburn Central), of Connersville, Ind. After 65,582 vehicles had been built, the now familiar jerry can bracket began to be installed on the left-hand side of the Jeep's rear panel. Like most of the World War II-era military vehicles, production of the MB ceased with the end of hostilities. Willys-Overland Motors had built 359,489 of the vehicles when production ceased.

The first 25,808 MBs had what is now known as a "slat grille." This was a welded assembly of heavy bar stock.

Vehicles produced after June 1942 used the now familiar lightweight stamped-steel grille, which is now the registered trademark of Jeep. Ironically, this grille had originally been developed by Ford for the GPW. The stamped grille was not only lighter, but also reportedly could be produced for about one third the cost of the fabricated unit it replaced.

The early models had "Willys" embossed in the rear body panel and are known as "script" Jeeps.

◆

Weight:	2,450 pounds
Size (LxWxH):	132" x 62" x 72"
Max Speed:	65 mph
Range:	285 miles

◆

Evelyn Harless

Condition code	6	5	4	3	2	1	Scarcity
Value (dollars)	800	4,500	9,000	12,000	16,000	20,000	1

Ford GPW

With the Jeep's design having been standardized as that of the Willys MB, a second source of supply was sought. Ford was licensed to build copies of the Willys design, to which Ford assigned its model designation GPW. Again, G meant government contract vehicle, P indicated it was an 80-inch wheelbase reconnaissance car and the W suffix indicated it used the Willys-designed engine.

Like the MB, earliest models had the maker's name embossed in script on the rear panel. The grille was of fabricated steel construction until Jan. 6, 1942. Then Ford introduced the stamped steel grille, which was later ironically registered as a trademark for Chrysler's Jeep.

Ford built its own bodies at the Lincoln plant until the fall of 1943. Then Ford began buying bodies from American Central, which was already supplying bodies to Willys. After only a short time, representatives of Ford, Willys and the Ordnance Department met and created the composite body, which incorporated the best features of each maker's body. This body is what is now known as the composite body,

and it was used by both Ford and Willys from January 1944 onward, although a few were used during the last months of 1943.

Throughout the production of the 277,896 GPWs, Ford marked many of the components with the Ford "F" logo. Among these components were pintle hooks, fenders, bolts, etc. However, due to materials shortages, non-F parts were sometimes substituted on the assembly line.

The script Ford name on the rear panel was discontinued in July 1942.

As a rule, the most readily spotted difference between the MB and the GPW involves the front cross member. This is a tubular member on Willys vehicles, and an inverted U-channel on the Ford.

Ford built the GPW at six plants: Louisville, Dallas, Edgewater, Richmond, Calif., Chester, Pa., and of course Ford's huge Rouge complex.

Weight:	2,450 pounds
Size (LxWxH):	132" x 62" x 72"
Max Speed:	65 mph
Range:	285 miles

Condition code	6	5	4	3	2	1	Scarcity
Value (dollars)	4,000	14,000	20,000	25,000	32,000	38,000	4

Wheeled Vehicles

GPA

America's Cup champion Roderick Stephens of the Sparkman and Stephens Co. designed the hull for the amphibious Jeep, as he did for the later, larger DUKW. Ford did the assembly work as well as the automotive engineering for this "Jeep in a bathtub."

Not only did the overhanging front and rear hull sections make the GPA longer than the standard Jeep, but the wheelbase itself was four inches longer than its non-amphibious brother. On the bow of the vehicle was a hinged splash shield for use in water and a capstan winch. The winch was driven via a pulley off the front of the engine. At the rear of the vehicle were a propeller and rudder, as well as the standard pintle hook.

Inside, the passenger compartment was much like a standard Jeep, with two individual seats in the front and a bench-type seat in the rear. Steps were recessed into the hull sides to permit entrance and egress to the vehicle.

The GPA was developed at the request of the Quartermaster Corps by Ford Motor Co., working with the National Defense Research Council.

Mechanically, the GPA is very similar to the GPW, with the same type engine, transmission, axles and transfer case, with only slight modifications to adapt them to the amphibious role. While Ford built the last of the 12,778 GPAs in 1943, unlicensed copies continued to be built in the Soviet Union for some time after that.

Weight:	3,660 pounds
Size (LxWxH):	182" x 64" x 69"
Top Speed, Land:	55 mph
Top Speed, Water:	5.5 mph

Karen Green

Condition code	6	5	4	3	2	1	Scarcity
Value (dollars)	1,000	3,000	6,000	9,500	13,000	16,000	3

M38

Even before World War II had drawn to a close, efforts were made to standardize as many components as possible to simplify supply problems, as well as to improve the overall quality of the vehicles.

Advancements such as 24-volt electrical systems, and waterproof ignition and a deepwater fording ability markedly improved the combat readiness of the vehicles.

Though work was begun in 1948, the M38 was always regarded as a stopgap vehicle. The M38 was slightly larger and heavier than its World War II MB

counterpart, but resembled its ancestor and used a powerplant very much like that of the World War II era "Go-Devil" engine. Still, with the increased weight of the vehicle, the flat head four cylinder was underpowered.

Continuing a pattern established earlier with the MA and MB, the M38 was given the Willys model number MC.

Weight:	2,750 pounds
Size (LxWxH):	133" x 62" x 74"
Top Speed:	55 mph
Range:	225 miles

Wheeled Vehicles

Evelyn Harless

Condition code	6	5	4	3	2	1	Scarcity
Value (dollars)	1,000	3,000	6,000	9,500	13,000	16,000	3

M38A1

Because of the increased size and weight of the M38 compared to its predecessors, performance suffered. A more powerful engine was desired. It was found in the F-head Willys "Hurricane" engine. However this engine was taller and the vehicle had to be redesigned to accommodate it. This resulted in the most profound difference between a base vehicle and its A1 successor in Army military history, the M38A1, or in Willys terms, the MD. The changes were so extensive that the new version was even given its own G-number, G-758.

Production of the M38A1 began by Willys-Overland Motors in 1952. Many scholars believe the M38A1 to be the last "real" military Jeep.

Willys Motor Co. stopped building the M38A1 in 1957. By the time production stopped, 80,290 vehicles had been produced for use by the U.S. military and an additional 21,198 units for other countries. M38A1 CDNs were built by Ford of Canada during the 1950s, then by Kaiser-Jeep in Windsor, Ontario in the 1960s. The Netherlands used its own domestic-built version of the M38A1. The Dutch-built Jeeps were assembled at the "Nederlandse Kaiser-Frazer" (NEKAF) factory in Rotterdam, in part using U.S.-made components supplied by Willys. The first of the 4,000 initial "Nekaf Jeeps" was delivered on May 28, 1955. When the last of the Dutch Jeeps was completed in 1962, almost 8,000 had been built.

Off-road performance of the Jeep was improved with the M38A1 by installing larger 7.00-16 tires, providing greater ground clearance, and the improved transmission, allowing easier shifting under adverse conditions.

The more powerful F-head engine allowed the new vehicle to handle the increased payload specification as well as keep up with the rest of the faster M-series vehicle family.

Weight:	2,665 pounds
Size (LxWxH):	139" x 61" x 74"
Max Speed:	55 mph
Range:	280 miles

Owned by Everette Doyle, photo by Joe Shannon

Condition code	6	5	4	3	2	1	Scarcity
Value (dollars)	1,000	3,000	7,000	12,500	16,000	20,000	4

M170 Battlefield Ambulance

A stretched version of the M38A1, the M170 was built designed as a front-line ambulance, though a few were used as radio trucks or airfield taxis. In the rear of the ambulance, a litter rack was mounted in the floor, an additional litter rack hung from the top bows on the right-hand side and a third was mounted behind the driver's seat. The passenger's seat cushion was removable and was to be stored on the windshield when using the upper right litter rack. In this manner it provided a cushion for the patient's head. Similarly, a small cushion was attached to the rear of the driver's seat. The passenger's seat back hinged forward and an extension attached to its back formed a protective cushion for the lower litter patient's head. The spare tire and fuel can were mounted inside the vehicle in a well to the right of the passenger's seat. A drop light on a cable reel was installed near the driver for use when treating patients at night.

In order to accommodate the long litters internally, the wheelbase of the M170 was 20 inches longer than that of the M38A1. The front seats of the M170 were narrower than those of a standard M38A1.

Production from 1953 to 1963 totaled 4,155 units.

Weight:	2,963 pounds
Size (LxWxH):	155" x 60.5" x 80"
Max Speed:	55 mph
Range:	300 miles

Evelyn Harless

Condition code	6	5	4	3	2	1	Scarcity
Value (dollars)	1,000	3,000	6,000	9,500	13,000	16,000	3

M151A1

For many laymen, indeed for many buffs, any 1/4-ton 4x4 vehicle is a "Jeep." But the final generation of vehicle in this weight class fielded by the U.S. military had its own name, the MUTT (Military Utility Tactical Truck). Developmental work for what would become the MUTT began in the late 1940s, even prior to the adoption of the M38. Both the M38 and M38A1 were considered interim vehicles until the improved model could be fielded.

Ford Motor Co. was awarded a contract to begin development of a new light utility truck. Light weight was a prime concern. To address this issue, Ford proposed various vehicle designs and materials. Ultimately, the unibody design won favor, and it was tested in both aluminum and steel construction. During trials, however, the lightweight alloy bodies developed stress fractures, and the idea was dropped in favor of a steel unibodied vehicle. The new vehicle, designated M151, was placed into production.

The rear suspension of the M151 was found to sometimes buckle or collapse, particularly when heavily loaded. This was often the case when the vehicle was burdened with mounted weapons and cargo. The redesign featured new high-strength rear suspension arms, with extra bump-stops. Production of the vehicles with this improved suspension, known as model M151A1, began by Willys Motors in December 1963. In January 1964, the name on the builder's plate of the M151A1s being produced was changed to Kaiser-Jeep Corp.

In 1964, a new round of bidding resulted in Ford regaining the 1/4-ton truck contract and Ford resumed production of the Mutt in January 1965. Ford's production of the M151A1 continued up through 1969.

Weight:	2,320 pounds
Size (LxWxH):	133" x 64" x 71"
Max Speed:	66 mph
Range:	288 miles

US Army TACOM LCMC

Condition code	6	5	4	3	2	1	Scarcity
Value (dollars)	1,000	3,000	6,000	10,000	14,000	17,000	3

M151A2

The M151 had a nasty tendency to roll over during sharp cornering, and its independent suspension often masked the oncoming threat until it was too late for corrective action. Realizing that increased driver training alone would not alleviate the problem, the military initiated another round of suspension redesign. This time the rear suspension system was completely redesigned. Rather than the independent "A"-frame used on the M151 and M151A1 suspension, a semi-trailing arm suspension system was used. This allowed maximum interchangeability of repair parts with the previous designs, as well as retaining many of the advantages of the independent suspension. The improved vehicle design was designated the M151A2. In addition to the redesigned suspension, other improvements including deep-dish steering wheels, larger "composite" type marker and tail lights, electric windshield wipers and a mechanical (as opposed to the earlier electrical) fuel pump.

Even though the new suspension reduced the tendency for roll-overs, in 1987 a Roll Over Protection System (ROPS) was introduced. This could be added to the vehicles to protect the occupants in the event of an accident. Unfortunately, the ROPS raised the center of gravity, exacerbating the tendency for rollover accidents. This is particularly the case if the ROPS is fitted to a MUTT earlier than the M151A2. The ROPS was never intended to be used on these earlier vehicles.

Production of the M151A2 began in 1969. Ford was the initial contractor, but in 1971 AM General was awarded its first MUTT contract. AM General went on to win all the remaining US M151 contracts through 1985. A short production run for foreign sales in 1988 marked the end of the MUTT-era. All the AM General built trucks were produced in South Bend, Ind. AM General was the successor firm to Kaiser-Jeep's military sales operations.

The Marine Corps continued to use the M151A2 as the basis for its Fast Attack Vehicle well after it had been phased out of service as a utility vehicle.

◆

Weight:	2,385 pounds
Size (LxWxH):	133" x 64" x 71"
Max Speed:	66 mph
Range:	288 miles

◆

Evelyn Harless

Condition code	6	5	4	3	2	1	Scarcity
Value (dollars)	1,000	2,000	3,500	6,000	8,000	10,000	4

M422 Mighty-Mite

The M422 was designed for the U.S. Marine Corps to fill the requirement of a small, lightweight, low profile, highly maneuverable vehicle. What the Marines got was a vehicle that did just that, and gave incredible off-road performance as well. The Mighty-Mite was developed by Mid-America Research Corp., but was perfected and produced by American Motors from 1959-63.

Only 1,250 of the original version of the M422 were built. Early models used a unique, and now hard to find, windshield.

The four-speed transmission was combined with a two-speed transfer case to shorten the driveline. All Mighty-Mites had limited slip differentials front and rear which, together with their short turning radius and light weight, gave them superb off-road performance. The limited slip differentials combined with

the center of gravity of the vehicle allowed it to be operated normally with either one of the rear wheels missing. For this reason, Mighty-Mites were not originally equipped with spare tires.

American Motors produced the Mighty-Mite before it owned Jeep. The Mighty-Mite was replicated as a popular children's toy at the time.

With an aluminum body, and an aluminum air-cooled 108 cubic inch V-4 engine, the Mighty-Mite weighed just less than one ton.

Weight:	1,700 pounds
Size (LxWxH):	107" x 61" x 60"
Max Speed:	62 mph
Range:	225 miles

www.dlbensinger.com

Condition code	6	5	4	3	2	1	Scarcity
Value (dollars)	1,000	2,000	3,000	5,000	7,000	9,500	4

M422A1 Mighty-Mite

An improved version of the Mighty-Mite, the M422A1, was built in larger numbers (2,672) than the initial model. The most apparent differences between the two models were the stretching of the body by six inches and the use of an M38A1 windshield. Viewed from the side, the additional ribs stamped into the flank of the vehicle to strengthen the lengthened area are obvious.

The wheelbase of the vehicle was correspondingly lengthened, resulting in the M422A1 having a 71-inch wheelbase vs. the 65-inch wheelbase of the earlier M422. The additional space was used to accommodate rear passengers. The additional length of the A1 was between the front seat and the rear wheelwell.

The same engine and transmission were used in both the M422 and the M422A1.

◆

Weight: 1,780 pounds
Size (LxWxH): 113" x 61" x 60"
Max Speed: 62 mph
Range: 225 miles

◆

Wheeled Vehicles

Half-Ton Trucks

Condition code	6	5	4	3	2	1	Scarcity
Value (dollars)	3,000	5,000	9,000	11,000	16,000	19,000	3

Wheeled Vehicles

Dodge Half-Ton WC-9, WC-18, WC-27 Ambulance

These trucks had the longest wheelbase of any of the half-ton Dodges. The long wheelbase and modified suspension combined to provide a smoother ride for the injured personnel they were built to transport. The box-like, totally enclosed, all-steel rear body was insulated and heated, and could accommodate four litter-ridden patients or six ambulatory ones. A folding rear step at the rear of the vehicle assisted in getting inside. Unlike most military ambulances, there was no partition separating the driver's compartment from the patient area.

Engines for the WC-9, WC-18 and WC-27 ambulances were the T207, T211 and T215, and the production quantities were 2,288, 1,555 and 2,579 respectively.

◆

Weight: 5,640 pounds
Size (LxWxH): 195" x 76" x 90"
Max Speed: 55 mph

◆

Crooked Creek Publishing

Condition code	6	5	4	3	2	1	Scarcity
Value (dollars)	2,000	3,500	6,000	8,000	13,000	16,000	2

Dodge Half-Ton WC-12

The WC-series trucks marked the beginning of the truly military-looking series of trucks that Dodge would build over the next two decades. Rather than the civilian look of the earlier vehicles, the WCs had a heavy grille and brush guard integrated into a single unit. This brush guard was rounded in the center, whereas the later 3/4-ton series trucks had a flat-faced brush guard. The hood, which sloped gently downward toward the front of the truck, was hinged in the center and opened from the sides.

Three different six-cylinder Dodge engines were installed in the vehicles of this series: the T207 217 cubic-inch, 85-horsepower engine, the T211, also 217 cubic inches, and the T215 230 cubic-inch, 92-horsepower engine. Regardless of engine installed, the transmission was a four-speed unit, while the transfer case was single speed. The half-ton trucks were not equipped with combat wheels.

The model number of each vehicle changed with the power plant installed and unique vehicle model numbers were assigned to winch-equipped vehicles.

The WC-1 was essentially a closed-cab pickup with express-type body with longitudinal seats and a T207 engine. Various other models of closed cab pickups were also built, including the WC-5 that differed from the WC-1 only by lacking rear seats.

When the engine of the WC-1 was upgraded to the T211, the model number changed to WC-12. More than 6,000 of these were built, making it one of the most common of the half-ton Dodges. The versatile Dodge was used by every branch of the U.S. military. The WC-14 and WC-40 were similar in appearance, but the WC-40 used the larger T215 engine, compared to the WC-12's 217 cubic-inch T211 straight six.

Open-cabbed versions of this vehicle were built as well, designated WC-13.

◆

Weight:	4,640 pounds
Size (LxWxH):	181" x 76" x 89"
Max Speed:	55 mph
Range:	300 miles

◆

Condition code	6	5	4	3	2	1	Scarcity
Value (dollars)	3,000	5,000	9,000	13,000	18,000	21,000	3

Dodge Half-Ton WC-23

The WC-23, like the WC-6, WC-7, WC-15 and WC-24, were Command Reconnaissance Cars. The unique, and now classic, body style of these vehicles was designed to permit ease of entry and exit by its ranking passengers. A folding table and map holder were mounted on the back of the front seat for use by the rear passengers. An easily removable canvas top and doors were provided for protection from the elements. The WC-7 and WC-24 had PTO-driven front-mounted winches. The similar appearing WC-8, WC-16 and WC-25 were officially designated Radio Cars. These vehicles had a large 12-volt battery box mounted on the right side of the body, which interrupted the running board with an antenna mounted above it, and radio equipment inside the vehicle. None of the Radio Cars had winches.

The hazard of the special design of the Command and Radio cars is that they were easily singled out as targets by opposing forces, a factor that led to their later elimination.

◆

Weight:	4,975 pounds
Size (LxWxH):	181" x 76" x 83"
Max Speed:	55 mph
Range:	300 miles

◆

Wheeled Vehicles

Condition code	6	5	4	3	2	1	Scarcity
Value (dollars)	1,700	3,500	5,500	7,000	10,000	14,000	4+

IH M-1-4

When the Marine Corps began shopping for trucks in 1940, it found that most of the Big 3 automakers' production capacity had already been committed to the U.S. Army. The Army's vehicular requirements were so large that there was little chance that any of the vehicles would be available to the Corps for quite some time.

The Marine Corps turned to International Harvester, the nation's number four truck builder, whose facilities were largely available. International assigned the prefix M for military to the model numbers, the first digit is the truck's off-road rating in units of 1,000 pounds and the last digit is the number of driven wheels.

Production of the M-1-4 totaled only 1,123 vehicles. All these trucks were of open cab design. With provision for a canvas top only, there was no provision for sides or doors.

The U.S. Navy Medical Department used an ambulance variant of the M-1-4 throughout the war, but combat units phased out the half-ton cornbinder in favor of the one-ton M-2-4 relatively quickly.

John Adams-Graf

Condition code	6	5	4	3	2	1	Scarcity
Value (dollars)	1,000	1,500	2,800	4,500	6,000	7,500	3

M274 Mule

Widely known as the Mule, this vehicle's official name was "M274 Truck, Platform, Utility, 1/2 ton." But its versatile abilities, yet plain appearance certainly made its Mechanical Mule name appropriate. Four different companies produced six different varieties of Mule between 1956 and 1970. All M274 vehicles had four-wheel drive and the first five varieties could be driver-selected to be regular two-wheel steer or put into a four-wheel steer mode. However, the top speed of the Mule was only about 15 mph.

Two different versions of air-cooled engines, both rear-mounted, were used over the years to power the Mules. The engines were pull-started on the first five models with a rope. The first two models (M274 and M274A1) used the Willys A04-53 four-cylinder engine. All subsequent models used the A042 Military Standard two-cylinder engine, which on the final version, the M274A5, was finally equipped with an electric start. The retrofitting of A0-42 engines into earlier M274 and M274A1 vehicles created the M274A3 and the M274A4 respectively. The Mule was widely used by the Army and Marines in Vietnam.

The first five versions were made of magnesium; the last type (M274A5) was made of aluminum. The M274 had twice the cargo-hauling ability of a Jeep.

◆

Weight: 900 pounds
Size (LxWxH): 119" x 49" x 49"
Max Speed: 15 mph
Range: 100 miles

◆

Patton Museum, Ft. Knox, Ky.

Condition code	6	5	4	3	2	1	Scarcity
Value (dollars)	1,000	1,500	2,800	4,500	6,000	7,500	3

M274A5

Some Mules had recoilless rifles mounted on them, and some of the M274A5 versions had TOW (Tube-launched, Optically-tracked, Wire-guided) anti-tank missiles mounted on them, like the one shown here.

An unusual feature of the Mule involved the basket for the driver's feet and the movable steering column. If a lot of cargo was to be hauled, the steering column could swing up and the driver then walked behind it and the Mule was driven in reverse. Thus cargo could be placed where the driver would normally sit. Or, if the driver thought there was a danger of him being seen or shot, the steering column could be swung further down so that the driver could crawl along behind the Mule, driving it from the ground. The speed and gear controls were located so that the driver could easily reach them regardless of what the configuration was.

Willys began the work on what was to become the Mule during World War II, and was the contractor for the first production models. Later manufacturers included Bowen-McLaughlin-York and Baifield Industries. The defense division (now General Dynamics Armament and Technical Products) of bowling equipment and recreational products giant Brunswick Corp. produced the final two versions.

These vehicles could be operated normally with the right front tire missing.

◆

Weight: 900 pounds
Size (LxWxH): 119" x 49" x 49"
Max Speed: 15 mph
Range: 100 miles

◆

Three-Quarter Ton Trucks

Condition code	6	5	4	3	2	1	Scarcity
Value (dollars) WC-51	1,750	3,250	7,000	10,000	15,000	18,000	1
Value (dollars) WC-52	2,000	3,500	7,500	11,000	16,000	19,000	1

Dodge WC-52 Cargo Truck

Second only to the Jeep in popularity with U.S. World War II vehicle collectors, the 3/4-ton Dodge is a classic.

These cargo trucks were all built on a 98-inch wheelbase chassis. The WC-51 was a basic cargo truck, while the WC-52 was the same vehicle, with the addition of a Braden MU-2 winch. Rather than using frame extensions to accomplish this as did the postwar M37, the WC series did this by using a longer frame.

Production of this series began in June 1942 at Dodge's Mound Road plant and continued for the duration of the war. These popular and durable vehicles were used by virtually every branch of every service, in addition to be being supplied to allied nations in large quantities. They remained in U.S. service through much of the 1950s and well beyond that in foreign nations.

In May 1943, a number of minor changes were made, including lower sides for the bucket seats, which made it easier to get in and out of the truck. In August 1943, a more noticeable change was made when the left front compartment was eliminated, visibly shortening the left side of the bed.

◆

Weight: 5,645 pounds
Size (LxWxH): 167" x 82.75" x 85.5"
Max Speed: 54 mph
Range: 240 miles
(Weights and dimensions given are for WC-51; for winch-equipped vehicles, increase weight 295 pounds and length 9 1/2".)

◆

Simon Thomson

Condition code	6	5	4	3	2	1	Scarcity
Value (dollars)	3,000	4,500	8,000	12,000	17,000	19,500	2

WC-54 Ambulance

This truck more closely resembles its 1/2-ton predecessors than the rest of the series, in part due to its rounded rather than flat hood. Production of the WC-54 began in 1942 and ended in April 1944. During this time, 29,932 ambulances were built, including 293 for the Navy. Unlike the vaguely similar carryall and radio trucks, the door windows of these trucks are a two-piece arrangement, including the main window and a vent window. Like the rest of the three-quarter ton Dodges, the WC-54 was used by the U.S. armed forces well into the 1950s, and even into the 1980s by allied nations.

In August 1942, the litter bracket was redesigned to better clear the spare tire housing, which is recessed into the driver's side of the ambulance body.

Sometime in mid- to late-1943, the fuel filler neck was enlarged to allow fueling from five-gallon "Jerry" cans, which necessitated slight changes to the left rear part of the body sheet metal.

◆

Weight:	5,645 pounds
Size (LxWxH):	194.5" x 77.75" x 90.375"
Max Speed:	54 mph
Range:	240 miles

◆

Wheeled Vehicles

Evelyn Harless

WC-55

The distinctive, military appearance, reliability and the ready availability of parts of the three-quarter ton Dodge has made it one of the most popular World War II-era trucks with collectors. These trucks were built in many varieties: cargo trucks, command cars, ambulances. The vast majority are lumped together under the Standard Nomenclature List number G-502. One vehicle of this family, however, was not part of the G-502 group, nor is it commonly found at shows. That is the G-121 Gun Motor Carriage. This vehicle was procured by the Ordnance Department, whereas the rest of the 3/4-ton Dodges were originally Quartermaster Corps responsibility until July 1942, when all Army vehicle procurement was transferred to the Ordnance Department.

After experimenting with both rear and forward-facing guns, the decision was reached that the weapon be rearward firing and on Sept. 25, 1941, the Ordnance Committee designated this vehicle as 37-mm Gun Motor Carriage T21.

Despite a few reservations, on Dec. 4, 1941, the T21 was recommended for standardization as the M6. On the day after Christmas, this was approved, as was procurement. In March 1942, the first production vehicle was delivered to Aberdeen Proving Ground.

As better vehicles became available, in 1943, the Ordnance Committee recommended that the M6 be reclassified as Limited Standard. At the same time it was ordered that all but 100 of the M6 Gun Motor Carriages in stock at the various depots at the time be converted to WC-52 weapon carriers.

This en masse conversion is one reason that WC-55s are so hard to find today intact. Those that were converted to WC-52 standards can be identified oftentimes by their modified data plates. There are also usually various grind and weld marks on the body where various brackets were cut off and WC-52-style stowage added.

Pat Stansell

Condition code	6	5	4	3	2	1	Scarcity
Value (dollars) WC-56	1,700	3,500	8,000	12,000	17,000	19,500	2
Value (dollars) WC-57	2,000	4,000	9,000	13,000	18,000	20,000	2
Value (dollars) WC-58	3,000	4,500	8,000	12,000	17,000	19,500	4

WC-57 Command or Reconnaissance Car

The style of these vehicles has made them very sought after by collectors and movie producers. It seems anyone with any importance in a war movie must ride in one of these trucks, probably because the open top allows the star to be seen and the dual bench seat creates a chauffeur-driven look. For the military, however, the purpose of this vehicle was to convey officers while providing them with an excellent field of view of the battle zone.

The WC-56 did not have a winch, while the harder to find WC-57 used the same MU-2 that was mounted on the WC-52 cargo trucks. The third variant, the WC-58, was essentially a WC-56 equipped with a full suite of radio equipment in the back seat and a new data plate. Only 2,344 of the WC-58 were built, making these the scarcest of the Dodge 3/4-ton command-type vehicles. Production of all these command-type trucks was discontinued in April 1944, in part due to their distinct appearance, drawing unwanted attention from the enemy.

◆

Weight: 5,375 pounds
Size (LxWxH) 167" x 82.75" x 85.5"
Max Speed: 54 mph
Range: 240 miles
(Weights and dimensions given are for WC-56 and WC-58; for winch-equipped WC-57, increase weight 295 pounds and length 9 1/2".)

◆

Wheeled Vehicles

Pat Stansell

Condition code	6	5	4	3	2	1	Scarcity
Value (dollars)	2,000	4,500	9,000	14,000	19,000	21,500	4

WC-64 Knock Down Ambulance

The boxy steel body of the WC-54 ambulance, while giving some measure of comfort for the patients, took up considerable precious cargo space in wartime ship convoys. As a compromise, the WC-64 "Knock Down" ambulance was introduced. The WC-64 could be shipped "knocked down," or partially disassembled, in considerably less space than the solid bodied WC-54. Contrary to rumor, these trucks were not meant to be disassembled once they were put together at their destination. These vehicles had a 121" wheelbase like the WC-54, but the Knock Down frame was reinforced, probably to compensate for the lack of body strength. These trucks were built from January 1945 until August of the same year, with the production totaling 3,500.

The canvas top over the cab was not readily removable. The Knock Downs were supplied with canvas doors with plastic windows, which could be stored in a canvas pocket on the cab top when not in use.

The lower part of the rear body was factory installed on the chassis, while the upper part was shipped boxed for field installation. The lower body had benches over the wheels, which were padded and could be used as seats by ambulatory patients. Alternately, they could serve as litter racks for the more seriously wounded. Under-seat storage boxes were provided on both sides fore and aft of the wheel wells. Like the other trucks in this series, the floor of the bed was made of hardwood. The upper, or knock down, portion of the box was steel sheathed wood construction, the inside surfaces insulated with cardboard.

There were two hinged litter racks provided in the upper section of the body, which could be sloped to the rear to aid in loading and unloading stretcher patients, or hinged downward to accommodate patients seated on the lower benches.

◆

Weight:	7,000 pounds
Size (LxWxH):	192.625" x 84" x 99.375"
Max Speed:	54 mph
Range:	240 miles

◆

Evelyn Harless

Condition code	6	5	4	3	2	1	Scarcity
Value (dollars)	500	1,500	3,000	4,500	7,000	9,000	1

Dodge M37

With the success of the World War II military Dodges, it was only natural that the Army turned to Dodge for an updated design in the late 1940s when the M-series vehicles were in their infancy.

These vehicles incorporated the lessons learned during the war, including the key M-series design elements of 24-volt sealed, waterproof ignition, improved weather protection, organic deep water fording ability and standardized ancillary equipment.

A synchronized transmission replaced the World War II-era crash box, and a two-speed transfer case was used, allowing manual engagement of the front axle as well as an additional reduction range. The six-cylinder engine of the WC-series was lengthened and reinforced for the new trucks. Steel doors with roll-up glass windows were a major improvement.

The M37 had a slightly lower silhouette than the World War II vehicles, a tactical benefit, and also were narrower, a definite improvement when operating off-road in wooded or rocky areas.

Production of pilot models for the new design was begun in the spring of 1950 and, in January 1951, mass-production began. The initial series production ended in January 1955.

The M37 tooling was placed in storage until February 1958, when it was dusted off and slightly modified to incorporate minor changes to accommodate a new style transmission and relocated spare tire mounting. The first of these new vehicles, designated M37B1, was completed in April of 1958. Except for 1960, the demands of the military, especially as the war in Vietnam escalated, were such that M37B1s were built every year through 1968.

The M37 family was the last series-produced medium weight specially-designed tactical truck purchased by the U.S. military until the advent of the HMMWV.

Weight:	5,687 pounds
Size (LxWxH):	184.75" x 73.5" x 89.75"
Max Speed:	55 mph
Range:	215 miles

Simon Thomson

Condition code	6	5	4	3	2	1	Scarcity
Value (dollars)	700	1,700	3,500	5,500	8,000	10,000	2

Dodge M43

Naturally, when the rest of the 3/4-ton truck family was updated, so was the ambulance. The M43 was the meat wagon of the G-741 series and, abandoning the lessons learned with the WC-64, reverted to a steel body. It was built on a longer 126-inch wheelbase chassis than was the cargo truck, and its suspension was designed to provide a smooth ride for its precious cargo.

Both the M43 and the M43B1 came with the spare mounted adjacent to the driver's door. This spare tire carrier was later incorporated into the B1 series of cargo trucks. No pintle hook was installed and, per Geneva Convention rules, no star or national symbol was incorporated into the vehicles' markings.

Weight:	7,150 pounds
Size (LxWxH):	195.625" x 73.5" x 91.875"
Max Speed:	55 mph
Range:	215 miles

John Adams-Graf

Condition code	6	5	4	3	2	1	Scarcity
Value (dollars)	1,500	3,000	5,500	7,500	13,000	21,000	4

R-2 Crash Truck

This diminutive fire truck packs a punch as big as its official title: Truck, Fire, Airplane, Forcible Entry, Type R-2. With the production total of a mere 308 units, the R-2 was never common. The bright red color, reflective markings and unusual shape make the R-2 stand out from the ordinary MV.

The R-2s were built by ACF-Brill on Dodge-built, government-supplied chassis. The trucks were designed to be used in conjunction with Type 0-10 or 0-11 Foam Trucks. The Foam Trucks were to provide a path to the fuselage through the flames, and the R-2 would supply the tools and equipment to access the aircraft interior and rescue personnel. The meager 20 gallons of bromochloromethane extinguishing agent (discharged not by pumping, but with nitrogen pressurization) would hardly fight a full-fledged aircraft fire, rather was intended to merely get the rescuers the last few feet to the victims.

The R-2 was built on a 126-inch wheelbase Dodge M-56 chassis. The government then provided the chassis (and two batteries each) to Brill for conversion into the R-2. These conversions were completed in 1956.

At the front of the truck is the standard 7,500-pound capacity Braden LU-4 PTO-driven winch as used on some M-37s, but in place of the standard hook, there is a grapnel. The winch is driven via a double-ended PTO on the truck transmission, the other end of which drives the 230-volt, 180-cycle, three-phase Homelite chain-driven generator mounted in the bottom of the rescue bed. This powers an electric circular saw, as well as the floodlights for rescue operations.

The glass in the cab doors is a special double pane insulating glass, and the arms that hold the windshield open are different than those on any other M-series vehicle.

The unusual sloping roof contains a model ID-1 11- to 20-foot extension A-frame ladder made by the Aluminum Ladder Company, which is accessible by opening the rear doors.

Swinging the rear doors open also exposes axes, pry-bars and a variety of other "forcible entry" tools stored on their interior surfaces. The open doors also provide access to two fire extinguishers, a Blackhawk model SB-52 porta-power, floodlight, nitrogen cylinder and the Mall circular rescue saw.

Cecil Jones vehicle, Evelyn Harless photo

MB2 Crash Truck

The ugly duckling of the 3/4-ton Dodge family is also the hardest to find. Built for the Navy in 1955 by the Fred S. Gichner Iron Works of Washington, D.C., the Dodge M56 cab and chassis they were based on was hardly recognizable. Equipped similarly to the R2, these vehicles were assigned to U.S. Navy bases.

A reported 200 MB2 were built, and only a handful survive.

Extremely hard to find, and value undetermined.

One-Ton Trucks

John Adams-Graf

Condition code	6	5	4	3	2	1	Scarcity
Value (dollars)	1,700	3,500	5,500	7,000	10,000	14,000	3+

IH Model M-2-4

The International Harvester M-2-4 truck was a one-ton, four-wheel-drive truck supplied to the Navy and Marine Corps during World War II. Production began in 1941 with an order for 584 cargo trucks. Most of these were open cab cargo trucks, but a few of these were built with closed civilian "K" cabs and military fenders and hoods. Seventy of the 584 trucks were equipped with winches.

Later orders brought the production total to 10,450 and, after the few closed-cabbed vehicles in the initial order, all were open cab cargo trucks. The open-cab M-2-4 trucks had very plain open cabs similar to those used on Dodge VC series 1/2-ton trucks with two bucket seats and no provision for a top or doors. The majority of the trucks were cargo trucks with a narrow cargo box, which further made them resemble the World War II Dodge half-ton models. A separate brushguard protected the actual grille and lights during off-road operation. The radiator cap protruded through a hole in the front of the side-opening hood.

The earliest production used civilian instruments, but those were supplanted in later production by the standard round military gauges.

◆

Weight: 5,820 pounds
Size (LxWxH): 197" x 84.5" x 89"
Max Speed: 45 mph
Range: 260 miles

◆

One-and-One-Quarter Ton Trucks

Wheeled Vehicles

Condition code	6	5	4	3	2	1	Scarcity
Value (dollars)	500	1,500	3,000	5,000	7,500	10,000	2

Kaiser M715

In a move opposite of the renowned $600 hammer, in 1965 the military opted for a militarized civilian vehicle rather than the custom designed and built vehicles that had been the norm since mid-World War II. Needing more trucks comparable to the M37, but hoping to save money by buying a truck that was in mass production, the M715 was born. This was an adaptation of the Kaiser-Jeep "Gladiator" pick-up.

The first production contract, for 20,680 vehicles, was awarded to Kaiser in March of 1966. Trucks began rolling off the assembly line in Toledo in January 1967. Additional contracts brought the production total to more than 30,500 M715 series trucks by the time production ceased in 1969.

The Gladiator tooling was used to create the grille, fenders, hood, doors and cab of the M715 family. Changes to the sheet metal stampings included opening up the upper part of the cab and doors to accommodate the military canvas cab top. Also, the front fenders were cut out to clear the military 9.00-16 tires. The new fold-down windshield resembled the one used on the M38A1.

The last of the M715 series to be built in Toledo were 43 prototypes ordered by the Army in December 1969. These M715s were slightly improved and intended for comparison tests against the Chevrolet XM705 1 1/4-ton truck design. Unfortunately for Kaiser-Jeep and Chevrolet, neither model was accepted.

The M715 was the first "M" series tactical vehicle to use primarily civilian commercial components. The cargo bed of the M715 was all new, unlike that of any other vehicle, military or civilian.

Weight:	5,500 pounds
Size (LxWxH):	209.75" x 85" x 95"
Max Speed:	60 mph
Range:	225 miles

US Army TACOM LCMC

Condition code	6	5	4	3	2	1	Scarcity
Value (dollars)	700	1,700	3,500	5,500	8,000	10,000	3

Kaiser M725

This was the ambulance variant of the family. The front sheet metal looked like a normal M715, but on the rear was an ambulance body very much like that installed on the M43 Dodge. From the firewall rear, everything about the M725 was different from the M715. A sliding steel door separated the driver's compartment and the rear patient compartment, which was equipped with four stretcher racks. Also provided on the ambulance body were a surgical light, air ventilators, double rear doors and a gasoline-fueled heater.

The M725 was found at bases stateside, in Germany and Korea, and reportedly some were used in Vietnam.

◆

Weight:	6,000 pounds
Size (LxWxH):	209.75" x 85" x 95"
Max Speed:	60 mph
Range:	225 miles

◆

Cecil Jones vehicle, photo by Evelyn Harless

Condition code	6	5	4	3	2	1	Scarcity
Value (dollars)	700	1,700	3,500	5,500	8,000	10,000	5

M726

This telephone maintenance truck was built on the same chassis as the M724. On its rear was a utility box body. However, this body differed significantly from the M724, for rather than being enclosed and mounting a generator/welder, it had an open cargo area in the back with outward facing storage compartments. This bed was much lower than the M724 contact maintenance body. Some of the M726s were equipped with the 8,000-pound PTO winch and had a spotlight mounted on the left corner of the cowling.

Weight:	6,500 pounds
Size (LxWxH):	220.75" x 85" x 80"
Max Speed:	60 mph
Range:	225 miles

Wheeled Vehicles

US Army TACOM LCMC

Condition code	6	5	4	3	2	1	Scarcity
Value (dollars)	2,000	3,000	6,000	8,000	10,000	12,000	3

M561 Gama Goat

Experience has shown that while traversing over rough terrain, trucks with rigid frames and limited suspension lose traction. In June 1966, the design was finalized as the M561 and was classified Standard A. LTV's contract was for development only and bids were solicited for a production order. In addition to LTV, bids were received from Kaiser-Jeep and Consolidated Diesel Electric Co., also known as CONDEC. CONDEC was the successful bidder and was awarded a contract for 14,000 vehicles at a government cost of $14,285 each. Production began in 1970 with the first deliveries in 1971, but the first units had so many problems they had to be returned to CONDEC for corrective work.

The production model of the Gama Goat had a foam-filled aluminum body with a steel tailgate, four-speed transmission, two-speed transfer case and limited-slip axles. Under normal conditions, the center axle drove the vehicle. The transfer case provided for engagement of the leading and trailing axles when conditions warranted. The shift lever linkages were complicated and somewhat delicate. This made driver familiarization as well as maintenance difficult.

The M561 was steered by the front and rear axles. The non-powered steering gear turns the rear wheels the opposite direction of the front wheels, and the rear wheels only move half as much as the front.

Weight:	7,300 pounds
Size (LxWxH):	226.6" x 80.4" x 90.8"
Max Speed:	55 mph
Range:	420 miles

Army Motors

Condition code	6	5	4	3	2	1	Scarcity
Value (dollars)	2,000	3,000	6,000	8,000	10,000	12,000	3

M792 Gama Goat

The Gama Goat was evaluated for use as an ambulance in February 1971 and an ambulance variant, known as the M792, was adopted as well.

The Gama Goat itself did not carry a spare. Instead, it carried a truss that could be used to disable the center articulation, allowing one of the intermediate axle tires to be repositioned replacing a flat. With the articulation disabled, the vehicle would not sag in the absence of the tire on the center axle.

The Gama Goat was powered by the Detroit Diesel 3-53 engine. The model number indicates three cylinders of 53 cubic-inch displacement each, yielding a total of 159.3 cubic-inch displacement for the engine. This engine produced 103 horsepower at 2800 rpm and 217 pound-feet of torque at 1500 rpm. For those restoring a Goat, the correct color for the engine when the Goat left the factory was Detroit Diesel Alpine Green.

In spite of the considerable research that went into this design, and its considerable innovations, the Gama Goat never lived up to its promise. By 1988, it was being phased out of the military's inventory. Unfortunately for collectors, very early in the disposal program the decision was made that the Gama Goat was to be demilitarized by destruction. Thus while many Goat parts are readily available, complete vehicles are difficult to get.

◆

Weight:	7,300 pounds
Size (LxWxH):	226.6" x 80.4" x 90.8"
Max Speed:	55 mph
Range:	420 miles

◆

US Army TACOM LCMC

Condition code	6	5	4	3	2	1	Scarcity
Value (dollars)	300	900	1,500	2,500	4,500	6,000	1

Dodge M880

These Dodges were a far cry from the proven World War II-era WC-series and the Vietnam-era workhorse, the M37. Rather than being purely tactical vehicles, the M880 series of vehicles were mildly militarized civilian trucks intended to provide the military with a low-cost non-tactical transport. The trucks were built by Dodge in 1976 and 1977 and, except for the ambulance, were essentially the contemporary Dodge commercial trucks.

The base vehicle of the series, the M880 pickup, was based on the Dodge 3/4-ton W200 pickup. A folding set of steel bows was available to support a cargo cover over the standard civilian bed. A form of the standard military folding troop seats was provided that would fit into the bed's stake pockets.

The trucks were powered by the standard civilian Chrysler 318 V-8, which drove the truck through an automatic transmission. The trucks also had power steering, and a civilian-type step bumper on the rear provided the mounting point for the pintle hook. A kit was available to add a 24-volt power system to the trucks. Most of the vehicles did not have military-type lighting systems, but a few had them added. Key versions of the series were: M881 had a 24-volt 60-amp generating system in addition to the standard 12-volt electrical system of the vehicle. With the addition of a communications kit, the M881 became a M882. When a S250 shelter was mounted inside the truck's standard cargo bed and secured with tie-downs, the truck became a M883. A truck with the S250 shelter, 24-volt, 100-amp electrical system and communications kit was known as the M884.

The M886 was an ambulance model using standard pickup sheet metal from the cab forward, but with an especially designed rear patient compartment. A sliding door in the rear of the cab allowed the attendant access to the heated rear patient compartment. A pair of double doors in the rear of the body could be opened for patient loading. Five litter patients could be carried.

Two-wheel drive variants of most models were produced as well.

Weight:	4,648 pounds
Size (LxWxH):	220.75" x 79.5" x 73.9"
Max Speed:	70 mph
Range:	225 miles

Wheeled Vehicles

Condition code	6	5	4	3	2	1	Scarcity
Value (dollars)	700	1,700	3,500	5,000	7,000	9,000	1

M1008 CUCV

Economics once again drove the U.S. military to become interested in commercial vehicles in certain roles rather than relying strictly upon tactical vehicle designs. In the post-World War II era, this was first evident with the Kaiser-Jeep M715, then the Dodge M880 series, and more recently the Chevrolet CUCV family of vehicles.

The Chevrolet Commercial Utility Cargo Vehicle series replaced the Dodge M880 series beginning in 1984. Like the M880, the trucks began with off-the-shelf civilian four-wheel drive vehicles, which then had some military components added. The militarization of the Chevrolets was fortunately a little more extensive than it had been with the M880 series.

The M1008 was the base vehicle of the CUCV series. It was essentially a diesel-powered version of the Chevrolet K2500, but used the front axle usually reserved

for the K3500 in the civilian line. At the rear of the truck was a standard step bumper with a pintle hook mounted in the center. The cargo bed itself differed little from the civilian model, but did have a lightweight folding cargo cover and removable troop seats added.

Modifications included the addition of a brushguard and towing shackles on the front bumper and a dual 12- and 28-volt 100-amp charging system.

The powerplant was GM's 6.2-liter diesel coupled to a TurboHydramatic transmission. Most models used the New Process NP208 two-speed, chain-driven transfer case. All models have non-slip rear differentials. The front axle had lockout hubs.

◆

Weight:	5,900 pounds
Size (LxWxH):	216.5" x 79.625" x 76"
Max Speed:	65 mph
Range:	270 miles

◆

www.tacticaltruck.com

Condition code	6	5	4	3	2	1	Scarcity
Value (dollars)	700	1,700	3,500	5,000	7,000	9,000	1

M1009

The M1009 was the lightest-duty member of the CUCV family. Based on the half-ton Chevrolet Blazer, it used the standard components rather than the heavy-duty suspension components of the rest of this series. The interior of the truck was essentially the same as that of its civilian counterpart, though lacking amenities such as air-conditioning, radio and carpeting. The interior upholstery was red vinyl, and originally rubber floor mats were installed, but these were later ordered removed because they trapped moisture.

Like the other vehicles in this group, it was powered by a GM 6.2-liter diesel engine and equipped with an automatic transmission and two-speed transfer case.

Weight:	5,275 pounds
Size (LxWxH):	216.5" x 79.625" x 75.5"
Max Speed:	65 mph
Range:	250 miles

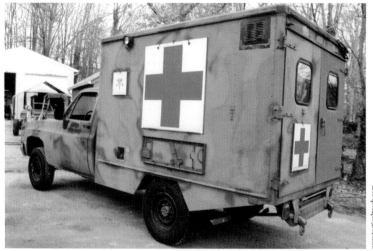

www.tacticaltruck.com

Condition code	6	5	4	3	2	1	Scarcity
Value (dollars)	700	1,700	3,500	5,500	8,000	10,000	3

M1010 Ambulance

The ambulance version of the CUCV series was the only member of the series that was factory air-conditioned. The custom-built patient compartment was not only heated and air-conditioned, but also was equipped with an elaborate air filtration system. A sliding door separated the driver's compartment from the rear patient area. A spotlight was mounted on the cab roof, and the patient compartment had an elaborate lighting system. The various lights as well as the air-conditioning and filtration required a lot of electricity, which was supplied by a 200-amp, 28-volt charging system.

The M1010 was also powered by the familiar GM 6.2-liter diesel engine. Its automatic transmission helped smooth the ride for patients.

◆

Weight:	7,475 pounds
Size (LxWxH):	222.5" x 79.625" x 101"
Max Speed:	65 mph
Range:	270 miles

◆

Wheeled Vehicles

www.tacticaltruck.com

Condition code	6	5	4	3	2	1	Scarcity
Value (dollars)	4,000	8,000	18,000	30,000	38,000	45,000	2

HMMWV

The affluent soccer mom's boulevard cruiser or the Army's standard light tactical vehicle, the HMMWV was born out of a 1979 desire to consolidate many vehicles into one. Teledyne, Chrysler Defense and AM General submitted prototypes of the new vehicle, which was to replace a menagerie: the M274 Mule, M151 MUTT and the M561 Gama Goat.

The Army dubbed this new vehicle family the High Mobility Multi-purpose Wheeled Vehicle, HMMWV. The soldiers called it the HUMVEE. After extensive competition, AM General was awarded the contract to build the vehicle in March of 1983.

The base vehicle of the HMMWV series was the M998. This vehicle could be configured as either two- or four-door, using removable panels. While most vehicles were supplied with a vinyl top and doors, they could also be equipped with a removable fiberglass top. The cargo area vinyl tops were supplied in a variety of styles, typically a low top that connected to the cab top and is the same height as the cab top. Also available was a high cargo cover.

When configured as a pickup, the backs of the rear seats, which are metal, are repositioned into a horizontal configuration and aluminum panels close the lower portion of the rear door openings. When configured in this manner, the "C" pillar is not raised and the rear cab panel is attached to "B" pillar. In this way, traditional troop seats can be installed in the rear of the HMMWV. The high cargo cover is used with vehicles configured to protect cargo and personnel from inclement weather. No spare tire is carried because the vehicles are equipped with run-flat tires and rims. Photos exist of vehicles with spare tires, but these were not produced for the U.S. government.

◆

Weight: 7,770 pounds
Size (LxWxH): 204.5" x 86" x 102"
Max Speed: 70 mph

◆

AM General.

Condition code	6	5	4	3	2	1	Scarcity
Value (dollars)	4,000	8,000	18,000	32,000	42,000	50,000	4

M1026A2

The M998A2 series, introduced in 1994, had numerous improvements in the power train. The engine was now the 6.5-liter (400 cubic-inch) diesel, and the automatic transmission was now a four-speed unit rather than the three-speed previously used.

The M1025 is an armament carrier without winch; the same vehicle with the winch installed is known as the M1026. This mount allows the HMMWV to be armed with a variety of weapons including the M60, 7.62mm machine gun, M2 .50-caliber machine gun or the MK 19 Grenade Launcher. The ring mount allows weapons traversal of a full 360 degrees. The vehicle shown here is a third series armament carrier with winch, or M1026A2.

◆

Weight: 6,780 pounds
Size (LxWxH): 204.5" x 86" x 76"
Max Speed: 70 mph

◆

Third Cavalry Museum, Ft. Carson, Colo.

M1114

While the war in Iraq brought great attention to the need for an "up-armored" version of the HMMWV, it wasn't an unknown concept. For some time, O'Gara-Hess & Eisenhardt has been producing the M1114 armored HMMWV, although the situation in Iraq brought about greatly increased production.

The M1114's roof-mounted turret can be used to mount the venerable M2HB Browning machine gun or more modern weapons such as the 7.62mm M60 or 40mm Mark 19 grenade launcher. Armor provides the crew with protection from 7.62 ammo at ranges more than 100 meters, as well as protection from antitank mines weighing up to four pounds. The roof is proof against aerial burst artillery rounds. Inside, a special lining protects the occupants from splinters. The 6.5-liter V-8 of the M1114 is turbosupercharged to offset the vehicle's increased weight, and the truck is equipped with an air conditioner so that the bullet-resistant windows can be kept closed.

◆

Weight: 12,100 pounds
Max speed: 78 mph
0-50: 17.84 seconds
This vehicle is not usually available to collectors.

◆

Wheeled Vehicles

AM General

M1097A2

The Special Forces uses an HMMWV especially adapted for its unique needs. The M1097A2 has supplemental armor that is resistant to a 44-grain bullet, a half-hardtop with ringmount for a M2 Browning machine gun or M242 Bushmaster, a brushguard, a front-mounted winch and a mount for an M60 at the co-driver's position. The bulk of these vehicles were produced by Letterkenny Army Depot (LEAD), where in an assembly line manner, standard HMMWVs were converted for use by Special Forces, Army Rangers and Navy SEALS. About 500 vehicles of this type have been produced.

This vehicle is not usually available to collectors.

Defense Department

Condition code	6	5	4	3	2	1	Scarcity
Value (dollars)	4,000	8,000	18,000	32,000	42,000	50,000	4

HMMWV with TOW

A key part of the initial design parameters of the HMMWV was to provide a means of transporting the TOW (Tube-launched, Optically-traced, Wire-guided) anti-tank missile system. Previously this had required two M151-series vehicles to transport (one for the weapon, and another for additional rounds), as well as the ubiquitous M2 HB machine gun.

Two different versions of the famous "slant back" HMMWV were developed to meet these requirements. The basic vehicle is the M1025/M1026 armament carrier, while the similar M966, M966A1 and M1036 versions transport the TOW missile system. The M1036 is a winch-equipped vehicle, while the M966 does not have a winch.

Both the armament carrier and the TOW missile carrier have four Kevlar-reinforced hard doors with polycarbonate windows and a metal, slant-backed roof. The armament carrier has a ring mount installed on its roof, while the TOW carrier has a specially designed mount supporting the launcher. This mount allows the weapon to be traversed 360 degrees, and through 20 degrees elevation and 10 degrees depression. The TOW can be dismounted and fired from a ground mount that is stowed on the rear of the vehicle, much like 40 years prior M3A1 scout cars carried tripods on their rear for dismounted operation of their machine guns.

From ground level, without the launcher installed, the TOW carrier closely resembles the armament carrier. However, a blast shield is installed to protect the radio antenna from the missile exhaust gasses. Internally, the cargo area is filled with racks to transport anti-tank rounds, which weigh about 50 pounds each.

◆

Weight:	6,780 pounds
Size (LxWxH):	204.5" x 86" x 76"
Max Speed:	70 mph

◆

One-and-One-Half Ton Trucks

Wheeled Vehicles

One and One-Half Ton Chevrolet Cargo Truck

Chevy produced about 160,000 of these ton and one-half all-wheel drive trucks during World War II. This chassis was quite popular with the Signal Corps, which used it as the basis for several of its vehicles, and more than half of the production was provided to other nations. Although the Chevy looks very much like a GMC 6x6 shorn of its rear axle, it is in fact a very different vehicle. These vehicles were built both with and without PTO-driven front winches.

A Chevy 235-inline six-cylinder engine powered the trucks through a four-speed transmission crash box. The two-speed transfer case (high and low range), which includes a provision to disengage the front wheel drive, completed the power train. Notice that the louvers on the engine side panels do not run the length of panel as they do on the GMC, but instead stop short. Banjo-style axles were used on the entire series.

The standard open military cab was never fitted to the Chevy. There was no provision for the installation of a machine gun ring mount.

Pat Stansell

Condition code	6	5	4	3	2	1	Scarcity
Value (dollars)	500	3,000	5,000	7,000	8,000	9,000	2

One-and-One-Half Ton Chevrolet Dump Truck

The dump truck version of the G-506 was equipped with a single-cylinder hydraulic hoist and sub frame. Two different brands of lift mechanism were used, but they were functionally the same. The bed itself was essentially the same as the cargo bed, but with a dual action tailgate that could be raised or lowered. These trucks were built on 145-inch wheelbase chassis. Over the years of production, Chevrolet assigned model numbers G7116, G4112 and G4162 to winch-equipped dump trucks, while non-winch model numbers were G7106, G4112 and G4152.

A handy size for small civilian contractors, once surplused, these trucks were snapped up by commercial users and oftentimes were completely worn out, making preserved examples difficult to locate today.

Weight:	7,545 pounds
Size (LxWxH):	224" x 86" x 106"
Max Speed:	48 mph
Range:	270 miles

Pat Stansell

Condition code	6	5	4	3	2	1	Scarcity
Value (dollars)	500	4,000	5,500	6,500	7,500	8,500	4

One-and-One-Half Ton Chevrolet Tractor Truck

G7113, G4112 and G4165 were the various model numbers Chevrolet assigned to its 1 1/2-ton 4 x 4 tractor trucks. Built on 145-inch wheelbase chassis, these trucks had a stationary fifth wheel and electric brake controls. Like the other members of this family (save the bomb service trucks), these tractors had hard top cabs and no provision for mounting an antiaircraft weapon, so their use was largely confined to rear areas.

◆

Weight:	6,140 pounds
Size (LxWxH):	206" x 85.75" x 87"
Max Speed:	48 mph
Range:	270 miles

◆

Condition code	6	5	4	3	2	1	Scarcity
Value (dollars)	500	4,000	5,500	6,500	7,500	8,500	4

Wheeled Vehicles

Chevrolet M6 Bomb Service

This is the only ton-and-one-half Chevy to be built with an open cab without doors or steel roof. The M6 was normally equipped with a small canvas roof covering the driver's compartment. In warmer areas, the canvas could be removed and the windshield folded down for ventilation. These trucks were designed to be used in conjunction with M5 Bomb Trailers on airfields to handle bombs. The trailers could be loaded using the hoist and monorail mounted on the rear of the truck. The Bomb Trailers, up to five at a time, were then towed out to the aircraft together.

The earliest trucks were equipped with Beebe chain hoists, while later trucks sometimes used a Holan hoist built by American Coach and Body Co. Braden winches were used briefly, but were found to be inadequate, and a modification work order was issued to replace them. These trucks were built on 125-inch wheelbase chassis.

Production of the M6 was suspended by the end of September 1944, its duties being fulfilled by the CCKW-based M27.

◆

Weight:	6,325 pounds
Size (LxWxH):	221" x 75.75" x 91.5"
Max Speed:	50 mph
Range:	432 miles

◆

Army Motors

Condition code	6	5	4	3	2	1	Scarcity
Value (dollars)	1,500	4,000	8,000	13,500	17,500	21,000	2

WC-63 Dodge 6x6

Compared to the creation of many of the military's vehicles, the genesis of the ton and one-half Dodge was simple. The army increased the size of a rifle squad from eight men to 12 men and, when that occurred, a squad would no longer fit in a 3/4-ton Dodge. Therefore, Maj. Gen. Courtney Hodges, chief of infantry, suggested the 3/4-ton Dodge be stretched 48 inches, and the vehicle became a 6x6. Most of the mechanical and some of the sheet metal parts were the same as those used in the 3/4-ton series.

Certain components, primarily in the driveline and suspension, were strengthened in the ton and a half models, and many of these changes were incorporated into subsequent 3/4-ton production as well.

The transfer was a dual ratio in the ton-and-one-half version vs. the single speed unit used on the 3/4-ton trucks.

The second version of the "Big Dodge" was the WC-63. It differed from the WC-62 only by incorporating a Braden MU2 winch. Like the WC-62, early models of the WC-63 had a Zenith 29-BW-12R carburetor, while later production used the Carter ETW-1 carburetor.

These vehicles are popular with collectors today because they have the "big truck" look with the ease of driving of a 3/4-ton truck. Additionally, their long wheelbase gives them a smooth ride, at least compared to that of other military vehicles.

A combined total of about 43,000 WC-62 and WC-63 trucks were produced. Although within the Chrysler Corp., the Fargo Division handled government contracts, the trucks were all built at Dodge's Mound Road truck plant in Detroit.

◆

Weight:	7,550 pounds
Size (LxWxH):	224.75" x 82.75" x 87"
Max Speed:	50 mph
Range:	240 miles

◆

Crooked Creek Publishing

Condition code	6	5	4	3	2	1	Scarcity
Value (dollars)	1,100	2,100	4,000	8,500	13,000	16,000	2

Ford GTB

These trucks, with their distinctive appearance, are known almost universally as Burma Jeeps. However, their base Ford model number was GTB. The style was originally developed as part of the Army's prewar low-silhouette truck program, but the vehicle was mass-produced for Russia as part of the U.S. foreign aid program. However, the Russians rejected the odd-looking vehicles, in part because their open cab was not well suited to harsh Soviet winters. Although these trucks have a very distinctive appearance, automotively they are very standard vehicles and use many off-the-shelf mechanical parts.

The driver sat alongside the engine, which was offset to the right. The passenger sat to the right of the engine, but unconventionally, the passenger did not face the front of the vehicle. Rather, the passenger faced the driver.

Production of these trucks began in mid-June 1942.

Although the Ford design was not well received by the Army, the Navy saw this truck as a way around the supply stranglehold the Army had on the G-506 Chevrolet of the same weight class. The Navy began negotiating with Ford in September 1942, ultimately becoming the primary user of these odd-looking trucks.

The first 6,001 vehicles were ultimately accepted by the U.S. Army. One thousand of the first 6,001 trucks were equipped with front-mounted PTO-driven Gar Wood winch.

Weight:	7,250 pounds
Size (LxWxH):	180.67" x 86" x 100.3"
Max Speed:	45 mph
Range:	440 miles

Two-and-One-Half Ton Trucks

Crooked Creek Publishing

Condition code	6	5	4	3	2	1	Scarcity
Value (dollars)	700	1,500	6,000	12,000	14,000	17,000	4

AFKWX-353

Production of this odd-looking "deuce and a half" began in 1942, and it was built alongside the more familiar CCKW in GMC's Pontiac, Mich., plant. These trucks were used in limited numbers by the U.S. military during World War II.

These trucks shared many mechanical components with the CCKW-353. The engine (except for intake and exhaust), transmission, transfer case, axles and cross members were all CCKW components. Even the canvas cab cover on the later open cab models was a CCKW part.

The big advantage these trucks had, in the eye of the Transportation Corps, was that even though the external dimensions were basically the same as the CCKW-353, the trucks had a larger cargo bed.

The first 60 of these trucks, with closed cabs and 15-foot steel cargo beds, bore registration numbers USA 492732 through 492791. Later trucks had closed cabs and wooden 15-foot cargo beds. Beginning in 1944, the truck and bed were lengthened by two feet, and the truck was designated the M427.

With only 7,235 of all types produced, the AFKW is one of the harder to find vehicles today.

◆

Weight:	11,950 pounds
Size (LxWxH):	289.5" x 86.25" x 106"
Max Speed:	45 mph
Range:	300 mile

◆

Pat Stansell

Condition code	6	5	4	3	2	1	Scarcity
Value (dollars)	500	1,200	5,000	8,000	10,000	15,000	3

CCKW-352

The GMC CCKW is generally considered to be the truck that won World War II. It was a medium-duty all-wheel-drive 2 1/2-ton truck. The CCW was an almost identical truck, lacking the front wheel drive.

The short wheelbase version was the GMC model CCKW-352, and the long wheelbase truck was known as the CCKW-353. The CCKW-353 was intended as a general-purpose cargo truck and personnel transport, while the CCKW-352 was built as a prime mover for the Field Artillery, towing 75mm and 105mm weapons.

Some of the trucks were built with winches. The cargo beds were initially steel, but in August/September 1942, the trucks began using wooden beds, and, finally in January 1944, a body of composite steel and wood construction began to be used.

The earliest models had fully enclosed cabs, but these were replaced in production during 1942 with the military standard open cab.

The earliest trucks all used axles built by Timken, which had a split differential design. As production levels increased, Timken was able to supply enough axles, and GMC was authorized to begin using axles of its own design in addition to the Timken units. Trucks built with the Timken axles have serial numbers ending in –1, while those with the GM axles have serial numbers ending in –2.

The earliest production trucks were equipped with a 25-amp, six-volt, positive ground electrical system, however in mid-1942 the trucks began to be produced with a 40-amp, negative ground system, still six volts. All these vehicles were equipped with vacuum-assisted power brakes, however two different styles of Bendix Hydro-Vac systems were used.

The CCKW was fitted with a greater array of body types than any other World War II era vehicles. In addition to cargo trucks, the following body types were among those installed, however this list is not a complete list.

Weight:	10,350 pounds
Size (LxHxH):	231" x 86.25" x 93"
Max Speed:	45 mph
Range:	300 miles

Pat Stansell

Condition code	6	5	4	3	2	1	Scarcity
Value (dollars)	500	1,200	5,000	8,000	10,000	15,000	3

CCKW-353 Closed Cab

The version of the CCKW that is most often remembered is the CCKW-353. As with the short wheel-based CCKW-352, the 353 came initially with a steel-roofed hard cab. The trucks were used for personnel transport, as well as general cargo transport in forward areas.

The six-wheel drive afforded excellent off-road performance compared to other contemporary tactical vehicles. Like other members of this family of vehicles, GMC's own six-cylinder 270 cubic inch powerplant was installed under the hood of this truck. A five-speed transmission, coupled to a two-speed transfer, completed the drive train. Ten 7.50-20 tires distributed the load, and the tractive effort to the ground.

A pintle hook attached to the rear crossmember permitted 7,500-pound on-highway or 4,500-pound off-road loads to be towed in trailers.

◆

Weight: 11,250 pounds
Size (LxWxH): 256.25" x 86.25" x 93"
Max Speed: 45 mph
Range: 300 miles

◆

Wheeled Vehicles

CCKW-353 Open Cab with Winch

Relatively early in America's involvement in World War II, the enclosed cab used on most vehicles gave way to a standard military open cab. Contrary to urban myth, this had nothing to do with steel conservation–in fact the open cab contained more steel than its closed counterpart. Rather, the advantages of the open cab were improved visibility and reduced shipping space.

The August/September 1942 conversion to wooden cargo beds, however, was an effort to conserve steel.

Some of the trucks, such as the one shown here, were built with 10,000-pound capacity PTO-driven winches.

Engine make/model	Gmc 270
Number of cylinders	6
Cubic inch displacement	269.5
Horsepower	91.5 @ 2750 Rpm
Torque	216 Lb-ft @ 1400 rpm
Governed speed (rpm)	2750

Wheeled Vehicles

Allied-Axis

Condition code	6	5	4	3	2	1	Scarcity
Value (dollars)	500	1,500	6,000	9,000	12,000	16,000	3

CCKW Dump Truck

At first glance, these trucks are easily mistaken for basic long-wheelbase CCKW cargo trucks. However, rather than a conventional bed, they were equipped with dumping beds. The dump bed is the same size as a conventional cargo bed, which often resulted in these trucks being grossly overloaded because their bulk cargo was typically much more dense than the personnel or crated cargo hauled in conventional trucks.

A moveable partition was provided in the dump body that was to be raised when used as a dump truck. This was to contain the load in the rear of the bed to prevent the truck from tipping over when the bed was raised loaded. However, oftentimes this partition was not used, and damage to the truck would result.

Both Gar Wood and Heil made dump beds for the CCKW.

◆

Weight: 11,950 pounds
Size (LxWxH): 272.75" x 86.25" x 110"
Max Speed: 45 mph
Range: 300 miles

◆

Crooked Creek Publishing

Condition code	6	5	4	3	2	1	Scarcity
Value (dollars)	800	1,500	6,000	9,000	11,000 16,000	4	4

GMC/LeRoi Compressor Truck

The U.S. Army Office, Chief of Engineers, began evaluating portable air compressors for use by engineer troops in the field in the early 1930s. By 1937, the decision had been reached to adopt a gasoline engine-driven, truck-mounted 105 cubic-feet-per-minute unit for issue to troops.

Fifteen days after Pearl Harbor, plans were drawn up for a factory-produced pilot model of the new vehicle to be assembled by LeRoi. On Feb. 24, 1942, an order was placed with LeRoi for 1,038 units, the first of several orders.

The model designation for this compressor was the LeRoi Model 105GA. The compressor was driven by its own four-cylinder, 318 cubic-inch engine, also built by LeRoi. The engine was joined to the compressor itself by a clutch. The compressor is a three-cylinder, two-stage, air-cooled unit with intercooler. It could deliver 105 CFM at 100 PSI. As adopted, the compressor and truck assembly, serviced and ready to work weighed in at 14,300 pounds.

In December 1943, an investigation was made regarding the desirability of equipping the compressor trucks with winches. The conclusion of this report was that a front-mounted, PTO-driven winch was desirable. Subsequently, winches were standardized on future procurements of these compressor trucks; in fact even to this day most trucks in engineer units are equipped with winches.

The other obvious change to the trucks was the substitution of the Studebaker-developed military standard open cab on the truck chassis beginning in 1942. The closed-cabbed compressor trucks were built on chassis using the Timken, or split-type axle, while trucks with open cabs can be found with either the Timken, or GM Corp. (banjo-style) axles. Beyond the initial order for 1,038 of these compressor trucks, a further 7,225 were ordered through May 1944, at a cost of $27.5 million including spares. On the final day of 1943, 2,020 of these were available in overseas theaters.

◆

Weight:	11,950 pounds
Size (LxWxH):	272.75" x 86.25" x 110"
Max Speed:	45 mph
Range:	300 miles

◆

Pat Stansell

CCKW Bloodmobile

The long-wheelbase CCKW-353 chassis was the foundation on which a number of specialized vehicles were built. In addition to the more common dump and compressor trucks, the CCKW was also the basis for aerial lift trucks, ambulances, machine shops, photographic laboratories, field hospitals, etc.

The Red Cross used the CCKW for mobile coffee shops, bringing a touch of home to troops, and for more serious work, such as this blood bank.

The venerable CCKW served in the military of many European nations through the 1980s, far exceeding its designer's expectations. These vehicles are too rarely found and traded to establish accurate values.

◆

Tire Size:	7.50-20
Fuel Capacity:	40 gallons
Electrical System:	6 Volt
Transmission	5 fwd, 1 reverse
Speeds:	
Transfer Speeds:	2
Turning Radius:	35 feet

◆

Wheeled Vehicles

Simon Thomson

Condition code	6	5	4	3	2	1	Scarcity
Value (dollars)	500	1,000	3,500	7,500	9,500	14,000	4

CCKW Tanker

In modern warfare, fuel has become as important a commodity as ammunition. Battles, if not entire wars, have been lost due to insufficient fuel supplies. Pipelines and tanker ships transported Allied fuel in bulk, tanker semi-trailers served some installations, but in many cases one of the final links in the supply chain was the CCKW fuel tanker.

Equipped with two 350-gallon tanks on the back that were flanked by long racks holding multiple "Jerry" cans, these trucks were never far behind the advancing tanks and armored vehicles as they crossed Europe.

Gravity was used to empty the main fuel tanks at the destination, whether redistribution or directly to the fuel tanks of other vehicles.

It is relatively difficult to find these trucks today with their original fuel tanks, as without proper maintenance they were quite susceptible to rust.

Condition code	6	5	4	3	2	1	Scarcity
Value (dollars)	3,000	5,000	10,000	14,000	18,000	30,000	4

DUKW

Though hardly sleek or stylish, the hull of this truck was designed by famed yacht designer and 1937 America's Cup winner Roderick Stephens. The automotive components were developed by GMC, based on its 2 1/2-ton, 6x6 model CCKW cargo truck. Though ungainly looking, the DUKW was outstandingly seaworthy. Though envisioned as a means to transport equipment and men from ship onto the shore, and some distance beyond, they were also used inland, notably during the crossing of the Rhine.

The DUKW was standardized in October 1942, and production began immediately at the Yellow Coach plant in Pontiac, Mich., which was also home to CCKW production.

Despite its successful demonstrations and tests, the DUKW was not fully appreciated by many in the military until after its successful use during the invasion of Sicily. After that, the DUKW's place in history was sealed.

Demand for the DUKW became so great that a second production facility had to be added, this one at the Chevrolet plant in St. Louis, Mo. Production totaled 21,147 vehicles by the time production ceased at war's end.

The name DUKW is an acronym for resulting from GMC model code: D indicates 1942 model year design, U is utility truck, amphibious, K for all-wheel drive, W for tandem rear axles.

Because of its unique abilities, the U.S. military did not phase the DUKW out of service until the 1960s.

Weight:	14,880 pounds
Size (LxWxH):	372" x 98.875" x 106"
Max Speed, land:	50 mph
Max Speed, water:	6 mph
Range, land:	240 miles
Range, water:	50 miles

Condition code	6	5	4	3	2	1	Scarcity
Value (dollars)	1,500	2,500	6,000	10,000	14,000	18,000	4

Studebaker and Reo US6 Trucks

Designed by Studebaker, which built the bulk of these trucks, the US6 was an alternative to the GMC CCKW and the International M5-H6 6x6 trucks. Studebaker's huge South Bend, Ind., works began turning out these vehicles in June 1941 and continued through August 1945. A total of 197,678 left what was once the nation's largest wagon maker. These were joined by 22,204 identical copies built by Reo Motors in Lansing, Mich. The Reo-built trucks were indistinguishable from the Studebakers, save for the data plates.

Regardless of maker, the US6 was powered by the Hercules JXD six-cylinder engine. This engine also powered the White M3A1 Scout Car and the Ford M8 and M20 armored cars.

Because so much of the US6 production was sent to Russia, which has notoriously harsh winters, the vast majority of these trucks have closed cabs. The irony of this is that the World War II Standard Military cab–used on almost every other truck–was developed by Studebaker! However, the weather prevented its use on all but about 10,000 of the Studebakers between December 1942 and March 1943.

These trucks were produced in short (148") and long (162") wheelbases. The US6 used the same transmission and transfer case as the GMC CCKW. Even the Timken axles were the same as those used on many of the GMCs.

The brake system employed by Studebaker was not the Hydrovac system that GMC used, but instead it was a vacuum-boosted system.

John Adams-Graf

Condition code	6	5	4	3	2	1	Scarcity
Value (dollars)	1,500	2,500	6,000	10,000	14,000	18,000	5

Studebaker and Reo US6x4 Trucks

In addition to the common 6x6 version, the US6 was also produced in 6x4 form. Since the 6x4 version was intended for on-road use only, its weight classification was five tons, whereas the 6x6 version was rated using the traditional off-road system of 2 1/2 tons.

The US Model was built with a number of body codes: U1 through U13.

US6Models

US6U1SWB cargo without winch

US6U2SWB cargo with winch

US6U3LWB cargo without winch

US6U4LWB cargo with winch

US6U5LWB 750 gallon tanker, with or without winch

US6X4U6SWB Semi-tractor

US6X4U7LWB cargo without winch

US6X4U8LWB cargo with winch

US6U9LWB cab and chassis without winch

US6U10SWB Rear Dump without winch

US6U11SWB Rear Dump with winch

US6U12SWB Side Dump without winch

US6U13SWB Side Dump with winch

US6X4 production stopped in July 1945, with the last all-wheel-drive version being built the following month.

Data for 6x6 version
Weight: 10,485 pounds
Size (LxWxH): 265" x 88" x 88"
Max Speed: 45 mph
Range: 240 miles
Value of 6x4 version

Photo by James Petralba, Fran Blake collection

Condition code	6	5	4	3	2	1	Scarcity
Value (dollars)	1,500	2,500	6,000	10,000	14,000	18,000	4

IH M-5-6

Although the first 500 of these International Harvester 6x6s were sold to the Soviet Union, these trucks are best remembered as the standard "six-by" of the U.S. Marine Corps in World War II. First produced in 1941, the trucks were assigned IH model number M-5-6 representing M-military, 5,000-pound capacity, six-wheel drive. The first 500 trucks were powered by the International FBC-318B 318.4 cubic-inch straight six-cylinder engine, driving through five-speed Fuller transmission and an International two-speed, four-shaft transfer case. Hendrickson walking beam suspension was used on all production models.

Once it was decided that the standard Navy and Marine Corps 6x6 was to be the International, some changes were made, the model then becoming M-5H-6. The engine was upgraded to the 360.8 cubic-inch FBC-361B, the rear axles were equipped with Thornton self-locking differentials and the tire size increased from the 7.50-20 tires previously to 8.25-20 tires. Most of the Marine vehicles were equipped with a 10,000-pound capacity PTO-driven front winch and an open cab. After producing 2,782 of these trucks, the engine was again upgraded, now using the RED-361B.

Most of the M-5-6 trucks were equipped with steel military cargo bodies similar to the steel beds used on the CCKW, but the later M-5H-6 trucks used a different style cargo bed, with a steel floor and either wooden or steel sides.

Rather than the rear-hinged hood of the US6 and CCKW, International used a center-hinged hood much like that of the 3/4-ton Dodge.

The locking differentials gave these trucks off road performance far superior to both the CCKW and the US6.

Weight:	13,400 pounds
Size (LxWxH):	270" x 88" x 98"
Max Speed:	46 mph
Range:	350 miles

US Army TACOM LCMC

Condition code	6	5	4	3	2	1	Scarcity
Value (dollars)	800	2,500	4,500	9,000	18,000	25,000	4

M34 Eager Beaver

Even before World War II had ended, the upper echelon of the Army had begun a series of studies that would bring about sweeping changes in all types of Army material. As a result of these studies, specifications were drawn up for a series of radically innovative transport vehicles with many advanced features. Because the new vehicles were so advanced, it was decided to field an interim series of vehicles, with an expected service life of less than 10 years. On Dec. 17, 1948, Joint Army Navy specification T-712 was laid down, representing these interim vehicles.

Reo Motors of Lansing, Mich., responded and a pilot vehicle was completed in 1949. By 1950, production of these vehicles was in full swing. Production of these "interim" vehicles finally stopped in the 1980's, and there are those in the military who say that its production should even now be ongoing.

The Reo-designed OA-331 inline six-cylinder 331 cubic-inch gasoline engine originally powered these vehicles. Later the same powerplant was license-built by Continental as its model COA-331.

The initial version of the new series was a 154-inch wheelbase cargo truck designated the M34. This wheelbase is known by the military as a long wheelbase truck. The M34 featured a 12-foot cargo box with wheel wells to accommodate the 11.00-20 single tires. The larger single tires were preferred over the dual-wheels of the CCKW due to their superior performance in mud and sand. Remarkably, this lesson seems to have been forgotten by the mid-1950s, only to be relearned in the 1990s.

The design of this truck has become synonymous with American military vehicles.

◆

Weight:	12,540 pounds
Size (LxWxH):	276" x 88" x 102"
Max Speed:	62 mph
Range:	350 miles

◆

Fred Crismon

Condition code	6	5	4	3	2	1	Scarcity
Value (dollars)	800	2,500	4,000	8,000	16,000	20,000	1

M35A2 Cargo Truck

A dual-wheeled version of the new truck was created for use primarily on roads (the single-wheel M34 being preferred for off-road operation). The dual-wheeled variant was the M35. Using dual 9.00-20 rear wheels, its cargo bed lacked wheel wells, providing a flat floor for loading cargo, although like the M34 it was equipped with fold-down troop seats.

In the late 1950s, the military was keenly interested in developing powerplants that could run on more than one type of fuel. Aware of this, Continental licensed M-A-N's "whisper engine" design that used a combustion process that Continental dubbed the Hyper-Cycle combustion process. After extensive tests, this engine was installed in the G-742 series trucks. This engine was a straight six model LDS-427-2 Multifuel engine, with 427 cubic-inch displacement. These engines are able to burn diesel, jet fuel, kerosene or gasoline, or any combination of these, without adjustment or modification. The adoption of this engine resulted in the truck being redesignated M35A1, and the slow-turning Multifuel engine required the regearing of the five-speed manual transmission into an over-drive configuration.

The M35A1 had a relatively short service life, being quickly replaced by the M35A2. With its improved 478 cubic-inch Multifuel engine, this would become the most common version of this family of trucks. Initially a LD-465 naturally aspirated engine was used, but soon environmental concerns forced its replacement with the LDT-465 turbosupercharged engine, known as the "clean burn" engine.

Through the years, Reo's 1949 design has been produced by no less than 10 companies, including Reo Motors, Studebaker, Studebaker-Packard, Curtiss-Wright, Kaiser-Jeep and AM General. Like all the early postwar vehicle designs, these trucks were equipped for fording with virtually no preparation.

◆

Weight:	13,860 pounds
Size (LxWxH):	276" x 96" x 112"
Max Speed:	58 mph
Range:	500 miles

◆

US Army TACOM LCMC

Condition code	6	5	4	3	2	1	Scarcity
Value (dollars)	800	2,500	4,000	8,500	18,000	23,000	2

M36 Cargo Truck

The M36, which many collectors refer to as a long wheelbase truck, is in fact an extra long wheelbase truck. Developed solely as a cargo truck, none of the 190-inch wheelbase cargo trucks are equipped with rear troop seats, but all have dual 9.00-20 rear wheels. The sideboards of the bed, however, somewhat resemble those of the shorter trucks. Like the 154-inch wheelbase M35, the 190-inch wheelbase vehicles were initially powered by the OA-331 gasoline engine. The right side of the bed of these trucks is a dropside design, swinging down to allow forklift handling of cargo.

The M36C was essentially the same truck as the M36, however in its cargo bed there were special appliances for transporting missiles.

The M36A1 was a Multifuel powered long wheel base cargo truck. It was powered by the LDS-427-2 and overdrive transmission.

When the 465 engine series engines were installed in the M36 and M36C-type trucks, they became the M36A2 and M36A2C.

All the cargo trucks, regardless of wheelbase, were available with and without PTO-driven front winches. The extended wheelbase of these trucks provides a noticeably smoother ride than that of regular cargo trucks.

Weight:	23,915 pounds
Size (LxWxH):	336" x 96" x 124.5"
Max Speed:	58 mph
Range:	300 miles

US Army TACOM LCMC

Condition code	6	5	4	3	2	1	Scarcity
Value (dollars)	800	2,500	4,000	8,500	18,000	23,000	2

M49A2C Fuel Tanker Truck

Fuel distribution was just as important in postwar planning as it had been during the push across Europe in World War II. Therefore, a fuel tanker was included in Reo's designs. Like the cargo trucks, through the years various versions were built. The M49, M49C, M49A1C and M49A2C each had a 1,200-gallon fuel tank body divided into 200-, 400-, and 600-gallon compartments. Access to each compartment was through a manhole, equipped with a manhole and filler cover assembly. Side skirts and running boards on each side of the tank body had sockets for mounting top bows and top tarpaulin with end covers to camouflage the fuel tanker as a cargo truck. The tank body sections could be filled or emptied by use of the delivery pump, which was mounted in the rear compartment. The pump was driven from a power take-off mounted on the transfer case. The delivery line gate valve assemblies and the two fuel dispensers with nozzle assemblies were provided to control the discharge of fuel. The tank body shell is extended beyond the rear tank bulkhead to form a pump compartment at the rear of the body.

The M49 did not have provisions for towing a trailer, but subsequent models did. Tanker trucks M49C, M49A1C and M49A2C were equipped with an aviation gasoline segregator kit. Tank trucks M49A1C and M49A2C were equipped with -427 and -465 Multifuel engines respectively.

The M49A2C did not have wheelwells made into the bed. All these trucks used a 154-inch wheelbase chassis and were equipped with 9.00-20 dual rear tires.

◆

M49A2C
Weight: 14,955 pounds
Size (LxWxH): 261" x 96" x 97.5"
Max Speed: 58 mph
Range: 500 miles

◆

US Army TACOM LCMC

Condition code	6	5	4	3	2	1	Scarcity
Value (dollars)	800	2,500	4,000	8,500	18,000	23,000	3

M50A1 Water Tanker Truck

Water is the most precious commodity for an army. Machines and, much more importantly, men must have a continuous supply of fresh clean water. Rarely are secure known safe supplies available. Many armies bring purification equipment with them, but that takes time to place in operation, and distribution is yet another problem. Water tank trucks provide a means of bringing fresh water with the troops and distributing water purified by the engineers.

The 1,000-gallon water tank body found on the M50, M50A1 and M50A2 water tankers was divided into 400- and 600-gallon compartments. Access to each compartment was through a manhole like that of the fuel tanker, but equipped with inner and outer manhole covers. Each compartment was filled through a filler cover and strainer. Delivery pump and valve controls were mounted in a rear compartment. Tank sections could be filled or emptied by the delivery pump that was driven by the transfer case power takeoff. Two delivery line gate valves, two water nozzles and three discharge hoses were provided to control the discharge of water. An insulated heating chamber below the tank connected to the engine exhaust system by the exhaust bypass valve, and the fording valve assembly protected the tank or pipes against freezing during severe weather. Like the fuel tanker, the running board and side skirts on each side of the tank had sockets for installation of the top bows and tarpaulin with end curtains for camouflage.

Weight: 14,955 pounds
Size (LxWxH): 261" x 96" x 97.5"
Max Speed: 58 mph
Range: 500 miles

Fred Crismon

Condition code	6	5	4	3	2	1	Scarcity
Value (dollars)	800	2,500	4,000	8,500	18,000	23,000	2

M109 Van Trucks

The successor to the World War II-era ST-6 van bodied truck was the M109 series. The M109, M109A1, M109A2, M109C, M109A3, M185, M185A1, M185A2 and M185A3 were all van trucks powered by the Reo OA-331 gasoline engine. The M109A2, M109A3, M185A1, M185A2 and M185A3 were equipped with the Multifuel engine. All the trucks had 12-foot van bodies, which were mounted on subsills to raise the body and eliminate the need for wheel housings. Two side-hinged doors were mounted in the rear of the body. The right door was equipped with a latch that could be padlocked. The left door could be opened only from the inside of the body. Ladders were provided for access to the inside of the van and access to the roof of the van. The body had side windows with screens and blackout curtains, and a front communication door. The bodies were wired for truck-supplied 24-volt DC or outside-supplied 115-volt AC power for lighting, accessories and tools. Heating and ventilating accessories were available to provide satisfactory working conditions in temperatures from 125°F. to -25°F.

Various shop sets could be installed in the van body. The body was waterproofed for fording to a depth of eight feet. All van trucks were initially equipped with hardtop cabs.

Weight: 15,291 pounds
Size (LxWxH): 263" x 96" x 130"
Max Speed: 58 mph
Range: 350 miles

US Army TACOM LCMC

Condition code	6	5	4	3	2	1	Scarcity
Value (dollars)	800	2,500	4,000	8,500	18,000	23,000	2

M275 Tractor Trucks

The short wheelbase chassis of the Reo-designed G-742 series was used for some dump trucks and the M275, M275A1 and M275A2 tractor trucks. These were 142-inch wheelbase trucks equipped with a fifth-wheel assembly mounted at the rear of the chassis. Air hose and electrical cable connections for semi-trailer service were stowed on the airbrake hose support that was mounted behind the cab. A deck made of nonskid plates bridged the frame between the hose support and the fifth wheel, so the operator could safely connect the intervehicular cables. Pioneer tools were stowed on a rack forward of the fifth wheel.

Air and electrical connections were also provided on the chassis rear crossmember, near the rear pintle, to allow for the towing of a standard trailer. The airbrake hand-control valve, used for semi-trailer airbrake control, was mounted on the steering wheel column. The M275 and M275A1 were not equipped with spare tire assemblies or toolboxes. The tools for these trucks were stored in the cab. A gasoline engine-powered M275, the M275A1 used the LDS-427 engine, and the M275A2 used various models of 465 Multifuel engine.

◆

Weight:	11,610 pounds
Size (LxWxH):	228" x 93" x 98"
Max Speed:	56 mph
Range:	320 miles

◆

US Army TACOM LCMC

Condition code	6	5	4	3	2	1	Scarcity
Value (dollars)	800	2,500	4,000	8,500	18,000	23,000	3

M292A1 Expansible Van

These van trucks were equipped with the M4 expansible van body. The expansible van body had two rear access doors and single access doors on either side of the body. Two ladders were provided for access purposes.

The single side access doors could be used only when the van body was in the expanded position. The expansible van body was designed to expand, under tactical conditions, to about twice the volume it enclosed when in the retracted or traveling position. This was achieved by expanding side panels, actuated by expanding and retracting mechanisms, and counterbalanced hinged roof and floor sections. All facilities, including lighting, heating, air conditioning and blackout protection, were available in both the expanded and retracted positions.

Four windows, equipped with brush guards, insect screens and sliding blackout panels, were located in each side panel. Two stationary windows were located in the rear doors. An opening designed to accommodate intercommunication facilities, normally covered by a removable plate, was located on the left rear panel toward the top. The telephone entrance jack and the auxiliary power cable entrance power were located on the left rear panel near the bottom. The pioneer tool bracket and power cable entrance receptacle were located on the right rear panel. A bonnet, extending from the front panel of the van, housed the two heating units and the air-conditioning unit. The electrical system included a 24-volt DC circuit for vehicular light operation, and 110-volt and 208-volt circuits for auxiliary equipment operation. The high voltage was supplied by a M200 trailer-mounted generator towed by the van truck.

The M292 was powered by the gasoline engine, the M292A1 was powered by the LDS-427 engine, and the M292A2 used the 465 Multifuel engine. All these trucks used a 190-inch wheelbase chassis and were equipped with 9.00-20 dual rear tires.

The great weight of these trucks, combined with their long wheelbase, make them the best riding of the 2 1/2-ton trucks on-road, but almost helpless off-road.

◆

Weight: 25,110 pounds
Size (LxWxH): 322" x 96" x 131"
Max Speed: 56 mph
Range: 500 miles

Memphis Equipment Co.

Condition code	6	5	4	3	2	1	Scarcity
Value (dollars)	800	2,500	4,500	9,000	18,000	25,000	3

M342A2

A major shortcoming of the World War II-era CCKW-based dump truck was its susceptibility to overloading. Its bed had sufficient volume to hold more cargo than it had the strength to support. When the new generation of dump trucks, the Reo-based M47 and M59, were introduced, they were on a short wheelbase chassis and had shorter beds to prevent this problem. However, in April 1953, Army Field Forces Board No. 2 tests reported that the M47 and M59 trucks were too small to accommodate a squad of combat engineers with full equipment, as desired. A secondary complaint was that they were too difficult to load and discharged their loads too close to the rear axle. Because it was impossible to correct these defects without a redesign, in

February 1954 the Ordnance Corps began a sub-project for the development of a new dump truck with an 11-foot body, to be designated the XM342.

Unlike the M47 and M59, which had one lift cylinder each, the M342 was equipped with two hydraulic hoist cylinders. The M342 used a 154-inch wheelbase chassis and were equipped with 9.00-20 dual tires.

◆

Weight: 15,665 pounds
Size (LxWxH): 260" x 96" x 105"
Max Speed: 56 mph
Range: 320 miles

◆

TacticalTruck.com

Condition code	6	5	4	3	2	1	Scarcity
Value (dollars)	800	2,500	4,500	9,000	18,000	25,000	3

M756A2 Pipeline Construction Truck

The M756A2 pipeline construction featured a body and auxiliary equipment mounted on a modified M45A2, 2 1/2-ton, 6x6, Multifuel engine equipped vehicle chassis with dual 9.00-20 rear wheels.

The body was an open top metal body with a wood-metal reinforced flat bed. This truck body was equipped with a winch and cab protector, rear mounted winch, two gin poles for constructing an A-frame, two 24-volt flood lights, a tailboard roller, a custom made tool box and stiff leg jacks for providing additional vehicle support. Weather protection for personnel and equipment was provided by a cargo body tarpaulin with end curtains supported by top bows. Front and side cargo body panels, removable for side loading, supported the top bows. The side cargo racks had built-in troop seats that allowed this truck to double as

a personnel carrier if need be. The body floor was equipped with provisions for mounting two sheaves, one located at the rear and the other toward the front of the body floor slightly off-center. Gin pole brackets were provided on each side of the body side frames for securing and carrying the gin poles that made up the A-frame assembly. Tailboard brackets were welded at each rear corner of the body side frames to accommodate the tailboard roller and allow for rear mounting and stowage of the gin poles.

A winch and cab protector was located between the cab and the pipeline construction body. The top portion of the winch and cab protector served as a platform to hold the gin poles during the raising and lowering of the A-frame. The rear winch was provided with 300 feet of 1/2-inch cable with a maximum capacity of 20,000 pounds on the first layer of cable.

US Army TACOM LCMC

Condition code	6	5	4	3	2	1	Scarcity
Value (dollars)	800	2,500	4,500	9,000	18,000	25,000	4

M764 Trucks

Earth-Boring Machine and Pole-Setter Trucks

These trucks were built for use by Signal Corps units when building communications lines. The body and auxiliary equipment were mounted on a modified M45A2 Multifuel chassis with dual 9.00-20 rear wheels. The rear of the frame had additional reinforcement compared to that of the cargo truck.

The M764 truck used a modified M35A2 cargo body with a clearance opening incorporated in the body floor for the winch mounting frame and boring machine mounting base. The rear winch assembly was mounted on the body behind the cab. The HDB2L earth-boring machine, which could bore a hole up to 30 inches in diameter, was mounted on the rear end of the body platform. The boring machine received its power from the power-divider and was equipped with two-way power leveling and a 16-foot rack bar.

The M764 body used the same bows, staves and body tarpaulin as the M35A2 cargo body. Stave pockets were incorporated between body side panels and staves. A cutout was provided in the front end curtain to fit over derrick tube. No rear end curtain was utilized because of the boring machine.

Hydraulically operated outrigger legs mounted at rear stabilized the truck during boring operations.

A two-section cab protector, attached to the M764 rear winch mounting frame, was a feature of these trucks. The upper section of cab protector was removable to reduce the overall height of the truck for shipping purposes. The upper section of protector also served as a support for the boring machine derrick tube, when the derrick was in traveling position.

All the M764 pole setter trucks were equipped with front winches.

US Army TACOM LCMC

M398 Lacrosse Launcher

While the 2 1/2-ton chassis has been used a platform for a variety of interesting trucks, most are relatively mundane service vehicles. Even when equipped with a ring mount and 50-caliber machine gun, the "deuce and a half" is hardly threatening. That is not the case with this version, however. Armed with a one-ton, 19-foot long Lacrosse missile, capable of carrying a nuclear warhead, the M398 could have dominated the battlefield.

The guided missile normally carried a single, 540-pound, shaped-charged warhead, although it could carry high explosive conventional, chemical as well as atomic warheads.

The operational vehicle issued was the M398 Guided Missile Launcher Truck, Helical Railed. The truck was based on the M45 154-inch wheelbase, gasoline-powered chassis with dual 9.00-20 rear wheels. The M398 vehicle became the operational mount for the Lacrosse Type I Guided Missile in 1958. With the launcher in the transport position, the M398 was 21' 11" long overall, 7' 10" wide and 9' 8" tall. The helical rail of the M398 launcher gave a 500-degree per second roll to the missile for improved accuracy.

Although issued to troops, these trucks were never used in a combat situation.

None known to be in private hands.

Dick Adelman

Condition code	6	5	4	3	2	1	Scarcity
Value (dollars)	800	2,500	4,500	9,000	18,000	25,000	4

530B Pumper

No less than six versions of fire truck were built on the Reo-designed chassis. The first class was the class 530, which was produced in rather small numbers, and had a front-mounted pump. The 530B, shown here, was developed in the late 1950s, using the M-44 single rear wheel chassis and a gas engine, as did the 530A. Only now the pump was at last mid-ships mounted (driven by a transfer case PTO) and the apparatus bed had compartments in which to stow the gear.

By late 1964, the 530B fire trucks were being built on a chassis with single 11.00-20 rear tires and the new Multifuel engine. Later production trucks used the dual rear wheel chassis with the Multifuel engine like the one in the photo.

With the use of the helicopter becoming widespread in Vietnam, there was a need to add aircraft crash and rescue to the Army firefighters' responsibilities. To aid in this, the truck was again updated, becoming the 530C. Improvements include replacing the 500 GPM Hale pump with a 750 GPM Waterous, adding a pump and roll feature, and the addition of a Feecon combination water and foam deck gun. Though appearing identical to the 530B, the body also changed slightly, becoming a couple inches taller.

The 530B and 530C saw extensive service in Vietnam, with the latter continuing to be used through Desert Storm.

Military fire service is a Corps of Engineers' responsibility, so these trucks were crewed by and issued to engineer troops, which were then attached to other units.

Wheeled Vehicles

US Army TACOM LCMC

Condition code	6	5	4	3	2	1	Scarcity
Value (dollars)	500	1,000	2,000	6,000	7,500	9,500	2

GMC M135

When Reo Motors with its G-742 (M34/M35 cargo trucks) was selected as the prime contractor for the "interim" series of trucks to replace the Army's aging fleet of CCKWs in 1949, GMC was dismayed. The company responded by submitting a prototype of its own design, built with corporate money, as an alternative. In its original form it had much in common with the CCKW, and this was a much-touted advantage. Many of the repair parts were already in place in the Army's supply channels and a minimal amount of new training would be required for mechanics.

Its most radical departure from the previous generation of vehicle was the installation of GM's Hydramatic transmission. The transmissions in these trucks had a rear pump. This allowed the truck to be pull-started in a conventional manner, something that can't be done with today's automatics.

The earliest trucks, the M135s, had 11.00-20 single rear tires for improved off-road performance.

The transmissions in the very first trucks shipped to Korea during that war were deficient. These problems were almost immediately corrected, but not before the transmissions earned an unwarranted reputation that lingers to this day.

Though these trucks did not garner the widespread acceptance with the U.S. Army that GM had hoped for, they did with the Canadian armed forces, where they formed the backbone of military transport for more than 30 years.

◆

Weight: 12,300 pounds
Size (LxWxH): 269" x 88" x 105"
Max Speed: 58 mph
Range: 300 miles

◆

Four-Ton Trucks

Condition code	6	5	4	3	2	1	Scarcity
Value (dollars)	2,000	6,000	10,000	12,000	16,000	19,500	4

Wheeled Vehicles

Four-Ton Diamond T Cargo Truck

While the classic style of the Diamond T makes it readily identifiable, less obvious and often understated is how near the military's postwar idealized 6x6 this truck came.

Initially known as the 969, the designation was changed to 969A when the instruments and filters were changed to the Military Standard type. The 969B was built for foreign aid requirements. They are most easily spotted by having only one each headlight and taillight, and having different paint.

All model 969 trucks were built with closed cabs. While the hood and fenders were engineered specifically for the military, the cab itself was based on Diamond T's commercial truck cabs. The 969A and 969B, on the other hand, were built in both open and closed cab versions, with military-style open cab appearing in the summer of 1943.

The Diamond Ts were powered by a Hercules RXC 529 cubic-inch straight six-cylinder engine. While the high torque engine combined with low gearing of the five-speed transmission (two-speed transfer case combination allowed an on-highway towed load rating of 12 1/2 tons), it also doomed the truck to a rated speed of 40 mph. The listed top speed and rated fuel consumption of three miles per gallon are both somewhat optimistic.

These trucks were built with a Bendix-Westinghouse air brake system, and a dual six- and 12-volt electrical system.

◆

Weight: 18,450 pounds
Size (LxWxH): 297" x 88" x 1195"
Max Speed: 40 mph
Range: 180 miles

◆

Pat Stansell

Condition code	6	5	4	3	2	1	Scarcity
Value (dollars)	2,000	10,000	12,000	16,000	25,500	29,500	3

Four-Ton Diamond T Wrecker

A formidable recovery vehicle was created by marrying the Diamond T chassis with the Holmes W-45 H.D. military wrecker bed. The bed was an adaptation of the standard Holmes W-45 twin boom civilian wrecker. According to Holmes' records, the first of the 6,420 G-509 wreckers, the model 969, was built in February 1941. The first unit carried serial #AB1-101; the final unit, shipped Oct. 24, 1949, was serial #AJ9-7339. The A in the first position of the serial number identifies the beds as a military W45 model.

The Holmes W-45 wrecker was a twin boom design with two five-ton winches mounted behind the cab. Each winch is equipped with 200 feet of wire rope. The twin boom design allows side recoveries to be made by swinging one boom to that side, and swinging and tying off the other boom to the opposite side to stabilize the wrecker. Stabilizer legs are mounted on each side of the bed, just behind the cab. Typical of US military wreckers, these trucks carried a lengthy list of recovery equipment, including chains, ropes, snatch blocks, cutting torches and tools. Unlike the later M series wreckers, which used the truck air brake system as an air source for tire inflation, etc., the W-45 left the factory with a self-contained air compressor mounted between the booms.

While not as powerful or versatile as the larger M1 and M1A1 wreckers, the classic styling of the Diamond T cab has ensured that these vehicles remain popular with enthusiasts.

Weight:	21,350 pounds
Size (LxWxH):	292" x 100" x 116"
Max Speed:	40 mph
Range:	180 miles

Pat Stansell

Condition code	6	5	4	3	2	1	Scarcity
Value (dollars)	2,000	6,000	10,000	12,000	16,000	19,500	4

Autocar U7144T 4x4 Tractor

Though in the minds of many enthusiasts the famed Red Ball Express was composed of endless streams of GMC CCKWs, in reality much of this priority cargo was hauled by trucks like this Autocar cabover tractor. Equipped with all-wheel drive, these truck tractors were used to tow a variety of semi-trailers, from flatbed to communications vans, in rear areas. The trucks were equipped with air brakes and trailer brake controls.

Like most World War II-era US-built tactical trucks, the initial production vehicles had closed cabs, but by 1942 production had switched to the military-style open cab. This greatly reduced the height of the vehicle. Autocar chose the six-cylinder, 529 cubic-inch displacement Hercules RXC gas engine as the powerplant for its cabover.

Popularly known today by its Autocar model number U-7144-T, the truck was assigned Standard Nomenclature List number G-510 by the Ordnance Corps. Autocar produced 11,104 of the Model U-7144-T.

◆

Weight:	12,360 pounds
Size (LxWxH):	203.5" x 95" x 112.75"
Max Speed:	41 mph
Range, empty:	540 miles

◆

Wheeled Vehicles

Pat Stansell

Condition code	6	5	4	3	2	1	Scarcity
Value (dollars)	2,000	6,000	10,000	12,000	16,000	19,500	4

Federal Tractor

Despite its totally different body, the Federal model 94x43 was operationally equivalent to the Autocar U-7144-T, even using many of the same major chassis components. The first Federals, the 94x43A, being based upon commercial products of the time, had enclosed cabs. Later models, the 94x43B and C, were redesigned to incorporate an open cab. When used by the Signal Corps, the 94x43 was referred to as a K-32. In Signal Corps use, the Federals pulled van trailers, while the transportation corps used them for general freight service. Federal built a total of 8,119 trucks of this type.

Kenworth and Marmon-Herrington were established as producers of these trucks late in the war.

◆

Weight:	11,950 pounds
Size (LxWxH):	203" x95.5" x109"
Max Speed:	40 mph
Range, loaded:	280 miles

◆

Five-Ton Trucks

Condition code	6	5	4	3	2	1	Scarcity
Value (dollars)	1,800	3,500	7,500	16,000	22,000	28,000	2

Wheeled Vehicles

TacticalTruck.com

M54A2 Five-Ton Cargo Truck

The genesis for the postwar five-ton 6x6 can be found in the June 1945 Cook Board Report and was affirmed by the November 1945 Stillwell Board Report, chaired by Gen. Joseph "Vinegar Joe" Stillwell. Both of these boards intended a design to have a five-year life span and the 1950 Army Equipment Board anticipated that the design would be replaced by cross-country carriers based on the T-51 design. Ultimately, however, the basic design continued production by various manufacturers until the 1980s.

International Harvester's design was selected for the "interim" vehicle, with one of the deciding factors being IH's engine choice: the Continental R6602. Continental Engines had previously tooled for a production of 3,000 units per month, an important consideration during the tense times of the Korean conflict.

However, in early 1959 OTAC (Ordnance Tank Automotive Command) ordered that the Mack ENDT-673 diesel engine be tested in the M54 truck. The ENDT-673 was a basically commercial engine of 211 gross brake horsepower at 2,100 revolutions per minute. It was a turbosupercharged six-cylinder valve-in-head water-cooled compression-ignition (diesel) engine.

In June 1962, the new generation of trucks powered with this engine was classified Standard A as the M54A1.

The installation of the ENDT-673 was short-lived, for after only a year it was decided to use Multifuel engines wherever possible in the tactical vehicle fleet. For the five-ton, the engine chosen was the LDS-465-1A. With the Multifuel engines installed, the model suffixes changed to A2.

Weight: 19,800 pounds
Size (LxWxH): 299" x 97.8" x 117.5"
Max Speed: 54 mph
Range: 300 miles

Memphis Equipment Co.

Condition code	6	5	4	3	2	1	Scarcity
Value (dollars)	1,800	4,000	8,000	17,000	23,000	29,000	2

M51A2 Dump Truck with Winch

As was often the case in World War II, in the postwar era dump trucks based on the 2 1/2-ton 6x6 chassis proved too light for many jobs. Therefore, a dump version was envisioned from the outset as part of the new five-ton 6x6 family. This vehicle, designated the Truck, Dump, five-ton, 6x6, was built on a 167-inch wheelbase chassis. It was equipped with 11.00-20 tires and dual rear wheels. A five cubic-yard capacity dump body and twin-cylinder hoist assembly was mounted on the rear of the chassis.

Like the cargo trucks, through the years the dumps went through a series of engine upgrades, their original Continental R6602 gas engines being replaced first with Mack diesels and then later the Multifuel engine.

These trucks were provided with troop seats and bows, allowing them to double as troop transports.

◆

Weight:	22,700 pounds
Size (LxWxH):	281.5" x 97.8" x 110.5"
Max Speed:	54 mph
Range:	477 miles

◆

Wheeled Vehicles

Joe Shannon

Condition code	6	5	4	3	2	1	Scarcity
Value (dollars)	1,800	4,000	8,000	17,000	23,000	29,000	2

M52A2 Tractor Truck

Used primarily by transportation companies and to a lesser extent by engineer and armored units, the M52-series vehicles were medium duty, off-road capable truck tractors.

The five-ton, 6x6, tractor truck M52 had a 167-inch wheelbase with 11.00-20 tires and dual rear wheels. A fifth-wheel assembly, approach plates and deck plate, suitable for hauling trailers, were mounted on the rear of the chassis. Tractor-to-trailer brake hoses and connections were mounted behind the cab.

Though conversion of these tractors to diesel power did not initially have the same priority as did the conversion of cargo and dump trucks, eventually they were repowered as well. The R6602 gas engine was supplanted by the Mack diesel, which in turn gave way to the LDS-465 Multifuel engine.

◆

Weight: 17,840 pounds
Size (LxWxH): 258" x 97.8" x 103.75"
Max Speed: 53 mph
Range: 477 miles

◆

M289 Rocket Launcher

The Honest John was a tactical nuclear rocket system developed the 1950s. A mobile launcher for the rocket was created on the M139 chassis, which had been developed for the M328 Bridge Truck. The earliest version of the launcher was the M289. These were built on the M139C and M139D chassis. Modified specifically for transporting the 7.62-mm rocket launcher, they had an axle gear ratio of 10.26:1.00 for increased tractive effort. Front axle loading was of great concern to the designers, therefore, in addition to reinforcing the axle housing, the front winch was removed from these trucks.

The M139D had a different rear axle and jack bracket supports and both the M139C and M139D had modified front cross-members. The M289 launcher had a long launcher rail that extended over the front bumper and was supported by an A-type frame at its outer end while traveling.

The later M386 launcher had a short launcher rail and did not require the A-frame support. The M386 was built on the M139F truck chassis that had a 6.443:1.00 axle ratio.

All the Honest John launchers were declared obsolete in 1982.

This is an extraordinarily difficult vehicle to find.

Condition code	6	5	4	3	2	1	Scarcity
Value (dollars)	1,800	4,000	8,000	17,000	23,000	27,000	2

M656

In the early 1960s, Ford was awarded a contract to produce a series of five-ton 8x8 vehicles. These vehicles evolved from the XM453E2 program. The production models were the M656 five-ton 8x8 cargo truck, M757 five-ton 8x8 tractor and the M791 five-ton expansible van truck. All of these models were also available with a front-mounted self-recovery winch. These trucks were typically used to support the Pershing missile system.

The XM656 had an eight-month testing program ending in 1964, which involved 40,000 miles of driving. These trucks were powered by Continental LDS-465-2 Multifuel engines, the most powerful version of the Multifuel to be placed into production. The engine was coupled to an Allison six-speed automatic transmission.

The XM656 differed from production models in details. The lifting shackle brackets were redesigned and a cup-shaped step was added to the front wheel assembly to make cab access easier.

These trucks had aluminum cabs and bodies, with the cargo body of the M656 having dropsides. Unlike similar looking civilian trucks, the cab did not tilt, rather, engine access was gained by removing a cover in the cab. Power steering was used to move all four front tires, and all eight wheels drove all the time through a single-speed transfer case. The trucks had air brakes, with outboard drums.

The M757 tractor had dual fuel tanks; the others had only one 80-gallon tank on the driver's side. The frame of the M791 was longer than that on the other vehicles, but the wheelbase and spacing were the same on all.

◆

Weight:	24,500 pounds
Size (LxWxH):	314" x 98" x 142"
Max Speed:	50 mph
Range:	310 miles

◆

Condition code	6	5	4	3	2	1	Scarcity
Value (dollars)	1,500	3,000	4,000	7,500	13,500	29,000	1

M813 Five-Ton 6x6 Cargo Truck

The M809 series of 6x6 five-ton cargo trucks was similar to the earlier G-744 series of five-ton 6x6 trucks. The principal difference involved powering the vehicle with a Cummins NHC-250 diesel engine instead of the variety of gasoline, diesel and Multifuel powerplants used in the earlier series. AM General Corporation performed the product engineering development as well as the production of these vehicles.

Production of the M809 series began by AM General Corporation in 1970 and continued into the 1980s.

The M813 was the basic cargo model and could carry five tons of cargo across country and 10 tons of cargo on roads. The foldable seats enabled 26 fully equipped troops to be carried.

The M813 truck had a 179-inch wheelbase, 11.00-20 tires and a 14- by seven-foot cargo bed. A PTO-driven 20,000-pound capacity winch was mounted at the front of some trucks.

◆

Weight:	21,461 pounds
Size (LxWxH):	304" x 98" x 116"
Max Speed:	54 mph
Range:	310 miles

◆

TacticalTruck.com

Condition code	6	5	4	3	2	1	Scarcity
Value (dollars)	3,500	5,500	9,000	14,000	20,000	36,000	3

M816 Medium Wrecker Truck with Winch

The medium wrecker M816 was used to return disabled vehicles for repair and to free mired vehicles. The vehicle crane, which was similar to the Gar Wood design used on the M543, could be used for lifting operations of up to 20,000 pounds. Common uses for the M816 as a crane were: (1) Removing and replacing engines, power packs and gun tubes. (2) Loading and unloading munitions.

The crane mounted was hydraulically powered, with the hydraulic pump being driven via PTO from the truck engine. The front and rear winches were both mechanically driven via PTOs from the truck's driveline. The front winch was used primarily for self-recovery if the medium wrecker were to become mired, or for assisting the rear winch by acting as an anchor point. The rear winch was the heavy-duty recovery apparatus and had a 45,000-pound pulling capability. Both the front and rear winches were equipped with level winding devices. The crane, which had a live boom that could be extended hydraulically from 10 to 18 feet was used for lifting loads up to 20,000 pounds. The rear suspension on the wrecker is different than that of the other trucks, having a beam above the springs to limit spring deflection.

◆

Weight: 36,129 pounds
Size (LxWxH): 356" x 98" x 114"
Max Speed: 52 mph
Range: 400 miles

◆

Condition code	6	5	4	3	2	1	Scarcity
Value (dollars)	1,500	3,000	4,000	7,500	13,500	29,000	2

M817 Dump Truck with Winch

Not surprisingly, the new series of vehicles included a dump truck. Designated M817, this truck was used to transport materials such as sand, gravel and stone or other bulk materials. These vehicles operated on or off the road with load limits up to 10,000 pounds.

When fully loaded, this vehicle could also tow trailers with loads up to 15,000 pounds. This vehicle had a welded-steel dump body that was lifted by two hydraulic cylinders. The forward end of the dump body extended up and over the vehicle cab to protect it and the driver from damage during loading. Troop seats were available, which allowed the dump truck to be used for troop transport operations as well.

The dump bodies on these trucks had a tailgate that could be opened at either the top or bottom, allowing operation as a regular (end load) type, rocker type or as a spreader type dump truck.

Weight:	24,426 pounds
Size (LxWxH):	288.5" x 97" x 116"
Max Speed:	52 mph
Range:	480 miles

Memphis Equipment Co.

Condition code	6	5	4	3	2	1	Scarcity
Value (dollars)	3,500	5,500	9,000	14,000	20,000	36,000	4

M819 Tractor Wrecker, Five-Ton, 6x6

This unusual vehicle was a combination semi-trailer tractor and wrecker. Intended to replace the earlier, similar M246-series vehicles, its primary purpose was the recovery of downed aircraft and helicopters. It was equipped with a hydraulically powered engine-driven crane, a front winch equipped with a level winding device and a fifth wheel for pulling a trailer. The crane, the boom of which could be extended from 11 1/2 to 26 feet, was used for lifting loads up to 20,000 pounds. The first section telescoped hydraulically, the second section did not have power extension. The boom was capable of 270 degrees rotation and approximately 45-degree elevation.

Whereas the M816 wrecker truck had a large rear drag winch of heavy recovery work, in a similar position the M819 mounted a fifth-wheel semi-trailer coupler. The base of the fifth wheel pivoted on a walking beam, which in turn pivoted on the sub-base. This construction permitted the fifth wheel to move in all planes. The M819 did not carry the extensive suite of heavy recovery gear found on the M816. The front winch was used to free the vehicle should it become mired.

Weight: 33,940 pounds
Size (LxWxH): 359" x 98" x 132"
Max Speed: 52 mph
Range: 200 miles

Keco Industries

Condition code	6	5	4	3	2	1	Scarcity
Value (dollars)	3,500	5,500	9,000	14,000	20,000	36,000	3

M923 Five-Ton 6x6 Cargo Truck

Development work on military vehicles is never complete. Even as production begins on one vehicle, work goes on to improve it. No sooner than the M809 five-ton 6x6 was type-classified, work began on its replacement. The areas targeted for improvements were the transmission, transfer case and brakes.

After extensive trials of the cargo and semi-trailer tractor prototype vehicles, in October 1979 the M939-series 6x6 cargo truck was type-classified. A production contract was awarded in April 1981 to AM General Corp. The M939 series was briefly built alongside the M809 series as one contract ended and another began. The basic cargo truck was the M923.

Rather than the air-over-hydraulic brakes used on U.S. 6x6s since World War II, the M939-series used commercial-type full air brakes. The air brakes were self-adjusting and backed by fail-safe mechanical spring brakes.

While retaining the conventional layout used by U.S. 6x6s, the M939 differed in some readily visible ways, especially in the area of the engine hood and the grille. The hood and front fenders were one unit and hinged to tilt forward. Thus, basic maintenance could be carried out from the ground, whereas even opening the hood on the earlier trucks required climbing onto the bumper.

Though the cab looked like the standard military one, it was considerably wider.

The engine used in the M923 and M923A1 was the 855 cubic-inch NHC250 Cummins similar to the engine used in M809 series.

Weight: 21,470 pounds
Size (LxWxH): 307" x 98" x 115"
Max Speed: 63 mph
:Range: 350 miles

John Adams-Graf

Condition code	6	5	4	3	2	1	Scarcity
Value (dollars)	3,500	5,500	9,000	14,000	20,000	36,000	3

M923A2 Five-Ton 6x6 Cargo Truck

While all the M939 and M939A1 trucks were built by AM General, which had developed the truck, a new contractor built the M939A2. In the mid-1980s, a team made up largely of former AM General employees put together the successful bid for the new series. Immediately after the award, the winners sold the contract to BMY, a division of HARSCO. Bowen-McLaughlin-York (BMY) of York, Pa., has a long and respectable record of building tracked vehicles dating back to World War II. However, this was the firm's first large-scale venture into building wheeled military vehicles. The BMY Wheeled Vehicles Division was established in a leased plant in Maryville, Ohio.

Rather than the 855 cubic-inch displacement naturally-aspirated NHC-250 Cummins engine used in previous trucks of the series, the M939A2 used a smaller turbosupercharged 504.5 cubic-inch diesel Cummins 6CTA8.3 engine. Horsepower ratings of the Cummins 6CTA8.3 are equivalent to the NHC-250.

Like the intermediate M939A1-series trucks, the A2-series vehicles rode on large 14.00-20 tubeless tires and single rear wheels, rather than the dual rear wheels that had been prevalent since the mid-1950s.

Size (LxWxH): 307" x 98" x 115"
Max Speed: 63 mph
Range: 350 miles

Bruce Kubu

Condition code	6	5	4	3	2	1	Scarcity
Value (dollars)	3,500	5,500	9,000	14,000	20,000	36,000	3

M928A1 Five-Ton 6x6 Cargo Truck

The M939-series trucks had extra-long wheelbase members, much like the previous M809 and M39 series. The M927 lacked a front-mounted, hydraulically driven winch, while the M928 was so equipped. Later, improved models of these vehicles bore the A1 and A2 suffixes like the rest of the series. These trucks had 20-foot cargo beds that did not include troop seats.

The engine in all of the M939-series trucks was fitted with connectors enabling to connect the new-at-the-time engine diagnostic equipment known as STE/ICE or Simplified Test Equipment, Internal Combustion Engine. The ease of use of this test equipment, it was hoped, would cut maintenance time and eliminate incorrect replacement of components based on poor diagnosis.

Weight:	24,300 pounds
Size (LxWxH):	383.2" x 97.5" x 115"
Max Speed:	63 mph
Range:	350 miles

Bruce Kubu

Condition code	6	5	4	3	2	1	Scarcity
Value (dollars)	3,500	5,500	9,000	14,000	20,000	36,000	3

M929A1 Five-Ton 6x6 Dump Truck

The dump truck member of this family is the M929 or, equipped with a front winch, a M930. Like that of most military dump trucks, the cab and its occupants were shielded from cargo during loading and transport by a substantial cab protector.

Like the rest of the M900-series trucks, the dump trucks went through the various improvements, including the A1 version shown here and, later, the A2 version. This entire series of trucks used a five-speed Allison Automatic transmission. This greatly simplifies driver training, improves off-road performance and reduces maintenance when compared the manual transmissions used in previous five-ton trucks.

◆

Weight:	24,300 pounds
Size (LxWxH):	383.2" x 97.5" x 115"
Max Speed:	63 mph
Range:	350 miles

◆

3 PG 15 PSB   HHD 118

M1078A1 Light Medium Tactical Vehicle

The Family of Medium Tactical Vehicles (FMTV) is divided into two groups, the Light Medium Tactical Vehicle (LMTV) and the Medium Tactical Vehicle (MTV). The LMTV is a 2 1/2-ton 4x4, while the MTV is a 5-ton 6x6. There is an 80 percent parts commonality between the two groups. Stewart and Stevenson of Searly, Texas, is the builder of this series.

The LMTV series consists of a truck chassis as well as cargo and van trucks with 12-foot bodies. In a departure from the practice used since World War II by the Army when describing the load capacity of medium tactical vehicles, the FMTV's on-road capacity is NOT double the stated capacity. Rather, the 2.5-ton rating of the LMTV is constant, and the truck is designed for use primarily on primary and secondary roads and trails. It is intended for line haul, local haul, unit mobility, unit resupply and other missions in combat, combat support and combat service support units. A complimentary trailer has been designed, which has an equal load rating and uses the same size body as the truck.

All FMTV variants were built to be capable of airlift in C-130 aircraft. Cargo variants are Chinook (CH-47) helicopter sling-load-capable, and there are variants specifically designed to be deliverable by low-velocity airdrop to meet the needs of airborne operations.

Weight:	17,589 pounds
Size (LxWxH):	253" x 96" x 112"
Max Speed:	58 mph
Range:	400 miles

M1083A1 Cargo

The Medium Tactical Vehicle (MTV) is a 6x6 with a five-ton payload capacity. The following models are available: 14-foot cargo (with and without materiel-handling equipment), tractor, wrecker, long wheelbase cargo and dump truck. These trucks are available with or without a midship-mounted winch. All versions are equipped with CTIS (Central Tire Inflation System).

The "A1" version of the FMTV includes a more powerful 1998 Environmental Protection Agency-certified engine, upgraded transmission, electronic data bus, an anti-lock brake system and interactive electronic technical manuals. The five-ton tactical trailers have the same cube and payload capacity as their prime movers.

In a notable departure from most previous U.S. tactical vehicles, the FMTV is a cab over engine design. This results in the typical FMTV vehicle being about 40 inches shorter than the vehicle it replaces, requiring less space for transport as well as improved maneuverability.

◆

Weight:	21,178 pounds
Size (LxWxH):	274" x 96" x 112"
Max Speed:	58 mph
Range:	300 miles

◆

Wheeled Vehicles

Third Cavalry Museum, Ft. Carson, Colo.

M1089A1 FMTV Wrecker

The heart of the M1089 FMTV wrecker is its dual 30,000-pound capacity recovery winch installation. Mounted on the rear of the vehicle is an 11,000-pound capacity wheel lift for use towing vehicles with damaged drivelines or suspensions.

A hydraulically operated material-handling crane with up to an 18-foot reach and up to 11,000-pound lift capacity is also mounted on the truck. Stabilizer legs are provided for use with this.

Like the other vehicles of this series, the M1089A1 is powered by a Caterpillar 3126 six-cylinder diesel engine. Its 330 horsepower are transmitted through an Allison MD 3070PT seven-speed automatic transmission. Michelin 395/85R20XML put the power to the ground.

The MTV and LMTV share common engine assemblies, although the LMTV has a lower horsepower rating. Other common components include cooling systems, transmissions, intake and exhaust systems, front axles and suspension systems, tires and wheels, cab assembly, vehicle control gauges and self-recovery winches.

Weight:	34,683 pounds
Size (LxWxH):	366" x 96" x 112"
Max Speed:	58 mph
Range:	300 miles

Six-Ton Trucks

Condition code	6	5	4	3	2	1	Scarcity
Value (dollars)	3,500	6,500	12,000	20,000	30,000	36,000	5

Six-Ton 6x6

This truck, bordering on obscurity, was ironically built by a greater number of manufacturers than any other truck in the U.S. Army inventory during World War II. Originally designed and built by Corbitt, of Henderson, N.C., production began in 1941. Corbitt assigned the vehicle its model number 50SD6. Soon, White began building identical vehicles with its own model number of 666 (six tons, six wheels, six-wheel drive). Both the 666 and the 50SD6 were intended as artillery prime movers. As such, they were equipped with midships winches and pintle hooks on both the front and rear crossmembers.

In 1942, Brockway joined in the manufacture of the six-ton trucks, assigning model number B-666 to its vehicles. While Corbitt's entire production was artillery prime movers, Brockway built longer chassis for Quickway cranes, pontoon and bridge-erecting trucks between 1942 and 1944.

Prime Mover production at White carried over from 1941 into 1942, when they were joined on the assembly line by plain chassis, bridge-erecting and gasoline tankers and truck tractors. In 1944, long wheelbase cargo trucks and chassis for Signal Corps vans were added to the line-up.

In 1945, yet another manufacturer, the FWD Corp. of Clintonville, Wis., began building this style six-ton truck. FWD completed 168 bridge-erecting trucks.

An 855 cubic-inch Hercules HXD six-cylinder engine powered these trucks.

◆

50SD6
Weight: 22,070 pounds
Size (LxWxH): 286" x 97" x 120"
Max Speed: 37.5 mph
Range: 200 miles

◆

Seven-and-One Half Ton Trucks

Condition code	6	5	4	3	2	1	Scarcity
Value (dollars)	2,500	5,500	9,000	14,000	18,000	25,000	5

Mack NO

One of the largest wheeled vehicles fielded by any army during World War II was this massive prime mover. Even 60 years later, modern military trucks do not dwarf this truck. The NO was a huge vehicle designed specifically to tow 155mm guns and eight-inch howitzers. Though the NO series was classified as a 7 1/2-ton 6x6, many of its components were also used in the production of the postwar G-792 10-ton trucks. The initial design, the NO-1, did not go into series production; rather it served as a test vehicle. The next version, the NO-2, went into production in 1943. A total of 403 of the imposing vehicles were turned out before production was shifted to the NO-3, of which 97 were constructed. These were followed by 1,000 of the NO-6 model. All the NO-3 and NO-6 trucks were supplied to overseas powers. The final incarnation was the NO-7, 550 of which were supplied to U.S. forces.

All the production NOs had wooden cargo bodies made by the Schantz Furniture Co. Any found with steel cargo bodies were rebodied during their lengthy NATO service. Another feature common to these trucks is the massive Gar Wood 5MB 40,000-pound capacity winch.

A hoist was mounted on the rear of the bed, which was used to lift the gun trails of the towed weapon during coupling. The hoist was also used to handle the two huge 12.00-24 spare tires carried in the bed.

But for the NO-1, all the NOs were nearly identical, differing only in details. The Mack EY, six-cylinder, 707 cubic-inch engine powering the NO developed 534 pound-feet of torque.

◆

Weight: 29,103 pounds
Size (LxWxH): 296.75" x 103" x 124.25"
Max Speed: 32 mph
Range: 400 miles

◆

Wheeled Vehicles

Ten-Ton Trucks

Crooked Creek Publishing

Condition code	6	5	4	3	2	1	Scarcity
Value (dollars)	2,500	5,500	9,000	14,000	18,000	22,000	4

M1A1 Wrecker

During World War II, the Army fielded a range of recovery vehicles, from tank-based tracked retrievers to the mighty M26 transporter. But the vehicle most often associated with "heavy wrecker" is the M1A1. Production of the earliest model of this series, the M1, began by Ward La France in 1940. Later, Kenworth was given a contract to produce a vehicle using identical essential serviceable parts, although the sheet metal work of the cab was different. A Continental Model 22R engine powered the trucks by both builders. Kenworth delivered its first M1 wrecker in mid-1942. Regardless of who built the chassis, the recovery equipment was built by Gar Wood Industries and included a crane with 180 degree traverse. In final form, production of which began in 1943, the trucks were designated M1A1. With the M1A1, the Series 5 Ward La France

and the model 573 Kenworth parts were completely interchangeable.

The M1 and M1A1, known at various points in their careers as six-ton or 10-ton wreckers, were the Army's standard wrecker until the 1950s, when the adoption of the M62 caused these to be reclassified as limited standard, before finally being phased out.

A limited number of the Ward La France chassis were used as the basis for the Class 155 Fire and Crash Truck.

◆

Weight:	30,000 pounds
Size (LxWxH):	348" x 99.5" x 117"
Max Speed:	45 mph
Range:	250 miles

◆

Wheeled Vehicles

US Army TACOM LCMC

Condition code	6	5	4	3	2	1	Scarcity
Value (dollars)	2,500	6,200	9,000	22,000	31,500	40,000	3

M123

Until recently, tanks have been relatively slow moving. They also have been, and still are, expensive to operate, both in fuel and maintenance. Every hour driven requires multiple hours of service. For these reasons, strategists prefer to haul the tanks as near as possible to the action. To transport disabled vehicles, some of the Army's largest vehicles have been built.

The first such series-produced vehicle in the post-WWII era was the Mack M123. Designed and originally produced by Mack, these trucks were initially powered by a throaty Le Roi V-8 gasoline engine with a whopping 844 cubic-inch displacement. These trucks produced a distinctive, ground-shaking sound. The five-speed crash box transmission shared a housing with a two-speed transfer case.

Production of the M123 10-ton tractor began in 1955. The tractors had either single or dual rear 45,000-pound capacity winches, and either low or high mounted fifth wheels. Mack had built 392 gas-powered trucks when production stopped in 1957.

In June 1965, Consolidated Diesel Electric Co. was awarded a contract for the first of what would be almost 3,000 diesel-powered versions of this truck. Known as the M123A1C, the truck used the same Mack axles and combination transmission and transfer case, but the engine now was the V8-300 Cummins. In June 1968, Mack re-entered the picture, receiving a contract to build 420 M123A1C trucks. At the same time, it was also awarded a contract to remanufacture 210 of the gas-engine driven trucks into diesel-powered vehicles.

The fifth wheels on these trucks accept 3.5-inch kingpins, and thus will not couple to normal semi-trailers.

These tractors soldiered on until the 1990s.

◆

M123A1C
Weight: 29,100 pounds
Size (LxWxH): 280" x 114" x 108"
Max Speed: 45 mph
Range: 350 miles

◆

Bruce Kubu

Condition code	6	5	4	3	2	1	Scarcity
Value (dollars)	2,800	8,500	11,000	25,000	34,500	45,000	5

M125 10-Ton 6x6

When the planners laid out the proposed post-World War II tactical vehicle families, the largest of the vehicles were to be the 10-ton vehicles of the G-792 series. Although several types were planned, only the tractor and, to a much lesser extent, the prime mover entered series production.

These trucks used many of the chassis components of the NO series 7 1/2-ton prime movers. As with the tractor, the massive Le Roi TH-844 V-8 gasoline engine powered the cargo truck. The vehicles used a non-synchronized combination transmission and transfer case that, along with the axles, were of Mack design and manufacture.

The M125 was produced for only one year, spanning 1957 and 1958. Like the NO before it, it was intended to tow 155mm guns and eight-inch howitzers. However the age of self-propelled weapons eclipsed the need for large wheeled artillery prime movers. Production ceased after only 552 units were built. All the M125s had a huge PTO-driven front-mounted 45,000-pound capacity winch.

◆

Weight: 31,600 pounds
Size (LxWxH): 331.5" x 114" x 111"
Max Speed: 42 mph
Range: 300 miles

◆

Twelve-Ton Trucks

Pat Stansell

Condition code	6	5	4	3	2	1	Scarcity
Value (dollars)	1,200	2,500	4,000	8,000	12,000	18,000	4

Diamond T M20

Originally developed to meet British requirements for a tank transporter, production of the Diamond T M20 began in 1940. Unusually for its size and intended purpose, the big truck lacked all-wheel drive and was just a 6x4. Perhaps even more unusual at the time was the choice of powerplant. Beneath the hood that stretched forward almost six feet lay an 895 cubic-inch Hercules DXFE diesel engine.

Just behind the cab a Gar Wood 5M723B 40,000-pound pull winch was mounted for use pulling disabled tanks onto the Rogers M9 trailer that was used in conjunction with this truck. A ballast box was mounted to the rear of the winch and above the tandem axles. Weight was added to this box to increase traction to allow the truck to pull the heavy loads without wheel slip.

The early trucks–Model 980–had 300 feet of wire rope for the winch. The later trucks–Model 981–had 500 feet of wire rope, and a pulley and fair lead arrangement that allowed the rope to be fed through the front bumper and used for self-recovery.

The powerful diesel engine drove the rear axles through a four-speed Fuller transmission and a three-speed Fuller auxiliary gearbox, which combined to give the truck the ability to pull loads well in excess of its 115,000-pound rated towing capacity. However, the deep gear reduction limited the truck's top speed to 23 miles per hour. Air brakes were used to stop the truck and its trailer.

When combined with the M9 trailer that was designed for it, the combination was known as the M19. Although widely used by the British, as well as the Soviet Union, France and other countries, the vehicle was never classified as Standard by U.S. forces. It was alternately Substitute Standard or Limited Standard, probably because of its non-powered front axle and use of a diesel engine. Diamond T records indicate 6,554 of these trucks were built. Despite a few reports to the contrary, no records exist that indicate that any powerplant other than the Hercules diesel were installed in these trucks as part of factory mass production.

Weight:	26,950 pounds
Size (LxWxH):	280" x 100" x 100.5"
Max Speed:	23 mph
Range:	100 miles

Miscellaneous Trucks

Simon Thomson

Condition code	6	5	4	3	2	1	Scarcity
Value (dollars)	3,000	4,500	8,500	17,000	20,000	28,000	4

M26 Pacific

The U.S. military issued a requirement for a vehicle capable of recovering disabled tanks in the desert, even under combat conditions. After several failed attempts by other builders, the military turned to the San Francisco-based Knuckey Truck Co. for a solution. Unlike others that had attempted to solve this problem, Knuckey was a small firm that specialized in building heavy-duty off-road trucks. The Knuckey design featured chain-driven rear wheels and was powered by a massive six-cylinder 1,090 cubic-inch Hall-Scott Model 440 engine. This engine had its origins in a 1930s marine engine Hall-Scott had developed.

While Knuckey's design impressed the Army, its production facilities did not. The Army felt that the Knuckey plant lacked the capacity to produce the number of the vehicles required by the war effort. Therefore, the Army awarded a contract to Pacific Car and Foundry of Renton, Wash., to further refine the design and place the vehicle into mass production. Pacific Car and Foundry assigned its model number TR-1 to the huge vehicles, though the firm's name Pacific is the name the vehicles are remembered by. The euphemism "Dragon Wagon" has been applied to a variety of tank recovery vehicles, but there is only one Pacific.

♦

Weight: 48,895 pounds
Size (LxWxH): 306" x 130.5" x 123"
Max Speed: 28 mph
Range: 120 miles

♦

Verne Kindschi

Condition code	6	5	4	3	2	1	Scarcity
Value (dollars)	3,000	4,500	8,000	16,000	18,000	25,000	5

M26A1

The mighty M26 had plenty of power and plenty of hauling capacity, but these attributes were sapped by the heavy armored cab. As the war progressed, recovering of disabled tanks began to be a lesser role for the trucks and the transport of tanks to the front gained importance. Therefore, an unarmored or "soft skin" cab was designed for the Pacific. Versions so equipped were designated M26A1.

Early in the production cycle of the Pacific, the critical labor situation in Pacific Car and Foundry's Renton, Wash., home (Renton was also Boeing's home) led to the truck production being relocated. Ultimately the truck assembly line was set up in buildings at the Midland Empire Fairgrounds in Billings, Mont.

Mechanically identical to the M26, the M26A1 lacked the heavy armored cab. In its place was a sheet metal cab with a soft top. Both vehicles had an M49C ring mount on the roof to support a Browning M2HB anti-aircraft machine gun.

After World War II, several vehicles were rebuilt to M26A2 standards, which included a 24-volt electrical system. These vehicles soldiered on into the 1950s with U.S. forces before being supplanted by the Mack-designed M123 10-ton 6x6 tractor.

Weight:	27,600 pounds
Size (LxWxH):	306" x 130.5" x 123"
Max Speed:	28 mph
Range:	120 miles

Verne Kindschi

M249/M250 4x4

This pair of trucks was developed specifically to transport the M65 280mm cannon, popularly known as the Atomic Cannon. For each M65 carriage, two 4x4 transporters are required, one each of the M249 lead unit and the M250 trailing unit. Kenworth Motor Truck Corp. built both transporter units at its Seattle, Wash., plant. Production spanned 1952-1953 and the first Atomic Cannon went into service in 1952. The last was retired in 1963.

The cannon was not fired while attached to the transporter. Rather, prior to firing, specially engineered hydraulic hoisting equipment on each of the trucks lowered the gun carriage and mount assembly to the ground. The trucks were then removed. After firing, the same equipment would lift and re-couple the gun carriage to the trucks. The two trucks could transport the weapon at speeds up to 35 miles an hour. The unit as a whole could move forward, backward or sideways since either tractor unit could pull while the other pushed, or they could turn at right angles to the center section and proceed parallel to one another.

The gross vehicle weight rating of the transporter was more than 85 tons. The cannon-transporter combination was 84 feet, 2 inches long.

Each tractor unit was powered by an Ordnance-Continental AO-895-4 air-cooled gasoline engine, which developed 375 gross horsepower.

A forward facing driver steered each truck, but the front driver controlled the throttle and the brakes of the entire truck-carriage-truck combination.

While no Atomic Cannons are in private hands, some of the power units are.

Jeff Rowsam

GOER

The desire to move large volumes of cargo over terrain generally considered impassable led to this unorthodox truck design. In 1956, the U.S. Armor Board began considering large wheeled earth movers as a basis for a possible new series of trucks.

Caterpillar was awarded a $5 million contract in 1960 to design, develop and build eight eight-ton cargo trucks. These test vehicles were delivered during 1961 and 1962. In June 1962, two 10-ton wreckers and two 2,500-gallon tankers were added to the contract.

In May 1963, a contract for 23 service test vehicles was awarded to Caterpillar. Sent to Germany in 1964 for extensive troop trials, then stored until 1966, they were ultimately sent to Pleiku, Vietnam, to support the 4th Infantry Division. Once in Vietnam, the GOER quickly proved its merit, being highly reliable and operating where no other vehicle could go.

Based on the positive reports from southeast Asia, in May 1971 Caterpillar Tractor Co. was awarded a production contract. This contract was for the purchase 812 M520 cargo vehicles, 117 M553 wreckers and 371 M559 tankers. Production began immediately, with final deliveries made in June 1976.

The GOER consisted of a front and a rear section. An articulated joint, that permitted lateral oscillation up to 20 degrees and a steering angle up to 60 degrees, connected these units.

The forward section had the cab, with seats for the driver on the left and the vehicle commander to his right, and the engine was behind the crew area. Power from the engine drove the vehicle via the six-speed transmission. The front wheel drive was full time, and the rear wheels were automatically driven in first and second gears but were automatically disconnected as the transmission shifted from second to third gear.

The cargo bed had side and rear doors to allow rapid discharge of cargo. These doors had watertight seals to preserve the GOER's swimming ability. The large cargo area could hold a CONEX container and two pallets.

Amazingly, these huge vehicles were fully amphibious. Water propulsion was via their wheels.

US Army TACOM LCMC

Condition code	6	5	4	3	2	1	Scarcity
Value (dollars)	8,000	16,000	18,000	25,000	32,000	45,000	4

LARC-V

The World War II-era DUKW was very successful at moving cargo from supply ships to points inland without port facilities, but the Army wanted something with greater capacity. The LARC filled this role. The "Lighter Amphibious Resupply Cargo" was much, much larger than the DUKW. Two different firms, Consolidated Diesel Electric and LeTourneau-Westinghouse, built slightly different versions of the LARC-V.

The engine was located at the rear of the hull and drove the vehicle through an automatic transmission. The entire body and hull of the LARC were made of aluminum and more resembled a wheeled barge than a floating truck. The cargo area was the large flat space on the center deck, and side curtains were installed to protect cargo from the surf if need be.

On the upper front of the vehicle was a crew cab that could be enclosed with either a hard or soft top. The steering controls were centered in the cab. The vehicle was quite complex and required extensive training to operate properly. The truck had hydraulic power steering. The engine was mounted in the rear of the vehicle, with the bellhousing toward the front of the vehicle. A single-speed transmission was connected to a two-speed transfer case that drove the four wheels by means of right-angle drives and planetary hubs.

The LARC was powered by a V8-300 Cummins diesel engine very similar to the engine in the M123A1C tractor. The load capacity of the LARC-V was five tons.

Weight:	19,000 pounds
Size (LxWxH):	420" x 120" x 122"
Max Speed land:	30 mph
Max Speed water:	9.5 mph
Range:	250 miles

Crooked Creek Publishing

Condition code	6	5	4	3	2	1	Scarcity
Value (dollars)	3,000	9,000	18,000	27,000	35,000	65,000	3

M911 Commercial Heavy Equipment Transporter

By the mid-1970s, the increasing size of new and proposed tanks pressed the limits of the capacity of the M123. The M746 had increased capacity, but was very expensive. The Army began investigating the possibility of procuring a new vehicle, based in whole or in part on a commercial vehicle. Oshkosh offered a truck tractor based on its commercial F2365 design. In September 1976, a contract for 747 of the vehicles, by then known as the M911, was awarded to Oshkosh.

The M911 is a very large 8x6 vehicle with an air-suspended helper axle. This axle could be lowered for better weight distribution when the truck was heavily loaded. The trucks were powered by a V8 Detroit Diesel engine, with the power being transferred to the axles via a five-speed Allison automatic transmission through a two-speed transfer case.

Behind the two-man steel cab there were two 45,000-pound capacity hydraulically driven winches for use when retrieving disabled tanks. Further back was a Holland four-way oscillating fifth wheel that accommodated 3 1/2-inch kingpins.

The wire rope on the rear winches was an inch in diameter.

◆

Weight: 39,952 pounds
Size (LxWxH): 369" x 98" x 140"
Max Speed: 43.9 mph
Range: 280 miles

◆

Crooked Creek Publishing

Condition code	6	5	4	3	2	1	Scarcity
Value (dollars)	600	3,000	4,500	8,000	16,000	18,000	3

M915, Tractor, Truck, 14-Ton 6x4

Beginning with the Kaiser M715, the Army has turned increasingly to using off-the-shelf civilian vehicles, or those based on them, for its transport needs.

The M915 is an example of this type of procurement. Created by AM General in response to a January 1977 request for proposals by the U.S. Army Automotive Material Readiness Command, it was based on the M915 on the Centaur series of trucks designed by the Crane Carrier Co. Deliveries of the 5,507 trucks, which spanned a four-year period, began in 1978.

Among the modifications made to the commercial vehicles to adapt them to military use were rear-mounted pintle hooks, front and rear tow hooks, and blackout lights and forest green CARC paint.

The M915 line haul tractor was powered by a 400-horsepower Cummins model NTC 400 6-cylinder diesel, driving through a 16-speed Caterpillar semi-automatic transmission. The truck's suspension was Rockwell-Asymmetrical leaf pin and shackle at the front, and Hendrickson RTE 380 walking beam on the rear.

The M915 became the Army's primary long distance hauler, usually pulling a 34-ton (U.S.) XM872 semi-trailer. In September 1981, AM General Corp. received a follow-up contract from the US Army Tank Automotive Command for 2,511 M915A1 (6 x 4) tractor trucks.

The M915A1 was a modification of the earlier M915 design. It was driven through an Allison HT 754 CR five-speed automatic transmission, and used 11.00-22.5 tires rather than the 10.00–20 of the earlier trucks.

◆

M915A1
Weight: 19,720 pounds
Size (LxWxH): 262" x 96" x 142"
Max Speed: 58 mph
Range: 315 miles

◆

US Army TACOM LCMC

Condition code	6	5	4	3	2	1	Scarcity
Value (dollars)	3,000	9,000	18,000	27,000	35,000	65,000	5

M977 HEMTT Cargo Truck

The GOER proved the need for a heavy transport vehicle, but was decidedly lacking in on-road performance. Accordingly, an improved vehicle was sought that would equal the GOER's off-road abilities and add to them high-speed highway performance. Toward this end, in May 1981 the US Army Tank Automotive Command awarded a $251.13 million five-year contract to the Oshkosh Truck Corp. for production of the 10-ton (U.S.) Heavy Expanded Mobility Tactical Truck (HEMTT). The first prototype was completed in December 1981 with first production vehicles delivered in September 1982.

The HEMTT design incorporated many components of Oshkosh's commercial truck line. These include the Oshkosh truck cab, standard eight-cylinder diesel engine and an off-the-shelf four-speed automatic transmission.

The base vehicle of the HEMTT family is the M977. Essentially very large cargo carriers, these vehicles include a light-duty hydraulic material handling crane at the very rear of the truck. The crane can reach any point inside the 216-inch long dropside cargo bed.

Some of the trucks have a 20,000-pound capacity self-recovery winch mounted near their center. The design is such that the winch can be used for self-recovery either to the front or rear of the vehicle.

The successfulness and utility of these vehicles was proven in the Gulf War and, subsequently with few improvements including installing armored cabs on certain vehicles, in the second Gulf War.

Weight:	38,800 pounds
Size (LxWxH):	400.5" x 96" x 112"
Max Speed:	62 mph
Range:	400 miles

John Adams-Graf

Condition code	6	5	4	3	2	1	Scarcity
Value (dollars)	3,000	9,000	18,000	27,000	35,000	65,000	5

M978 HEMTT Tanker

To keep pace with the rapid advance capability of the Army today, a high-speed, high-capacity and high mobility tanker was needed. The HEMTT fuel tanker, with its 2,500-gallon capacity and 62 mph top speed coupled with its eight-wheel drive, fills that niche.

Like the cargo version, the chassis is made of heat-treated carbon manganese steel that is bolted together with grade eight bolts. As do all HEMTTs, the M978 has a heavy-duty front bumper and skid plate, external hydraulic connection, service and emergency air brake connection, slave start connection and trailer electrical connector.

The tanker, which can be used to transport diesel or jet fuel, was built both with and without a self-recovery winch.

The powerplant selected for the HEMTT family was the Detroit Diesel 8V92TA V-8 diesel.

Weight:	38,200 pounds
Size (LxWxH):	400.5" x 96" x 112"
Max Speed:	62 mph
Range:	400 miles

US Army TACOM LCMC

Condition code	6	5	4	3	2	1	Scarcity
Value (dollars)	3,000	9,000	18,000	27,000	35,000	65,000	5

M984 HEMTT Wrecker

The recovery member of the HEMTT family is the M984. The Grove 14,000-pound capacity recovery crane with nine-foot boom at the rear of the truck allows the wrecker to lift one end of badly damaged vehicles or, in the case of smaller vehicles, suspend it completely. In addition to the standard HEMTT self-recovery winch, the M984 also has a 60,000-pound capacity drag winch. In order to make the vehicle even more self-sufficient, a small cargo area is provided to transport replacement power packs and other repair supplies.

All models of the HEMTT use the Oshkosh 46K front tandem axles, both of which steer. These axles include an inter-axle driver-controlled differential, and additionally the driver can disconnect the power to the front axles. Naturally, these trucks have power-assisted steering.

A variety of Eaton rear axles are used on the various HEMTT models. All are single reduction and have a driver-controlled differential.

◆

Weight: 50,900 pounds
Size (LxWxH): 392" x 96" x 112"
Max Speed: 62 mph
Range: 400 miles

◆

Wheeled Armor

Ron Grasso

Condition code	6	5	4	3	2	1	Scarcity
Value (dollars)	2,500	4,000	9,000	18,000	25,000	30,000	3

M3A1 White Scout Car

The debate of the merits of wheeled versus track-laying armor has raged since the early days of mechanized combat and continues today. Just prior to the U.S. involvement in World War II, the development of armored scout cars was a part of this debate.

The earliest M3A1s differed from later production models in various details. Initially, the "greenhouse" type windshield was retained. This system featured a protruding windshield with a side "wing" on each side. The windshield was designed to be folded forward when the armor cover needed to be lowered. Later production vehicles had the more familiar removable glass panels that were to be removed prior to lowering the armor cover.

Series production of the M3A1 Scout car began in 1940 and continued until March 1944. The White Motor Co. in Cleveland, Ohio, ultimately built about 21,000 chassis under a total of 13 contracts by the time production was discontinued. The Diebold Safe and Lock Co. fabricated and installed the armor plating, which was 1/4-inch thick and of the face-hardened type. After installation of the armor, the cars were driven back to the White plant for final assembly and inspection. Slightly more than half of these vehicles were supplied to other nations, primarily Russia, as foreign aid.

Armament was a variety of machine guns mounted by means of trolley and pintle to a skate rail that went completely around the interior of the fighting compartment. Today, this skate rail has often been removed or had the section above the doors cut out. Another frequent civilian modification is cutting a door in the rear armor.

The 86-horsepower Hercules JXD engine could drive it to 50 mph through its four-speed gear box.

◆

Weight:	91,00 pounds
Size (LxWxH):	221.5" x 80" x 78.5"
Max Speed	50 mph
Range:	250 miles

◆

Pat Stansell

Condition code	6	5	4	3	2	1	Scarcity
Value (dollars)	2,500	4,000	9,000	18,000	25,000	30,000	4

M8 Greyhound

Known to the British as the Greyhound, the Hercules JXD-powered M8 armored car's high speed was its best defense. The welded armored hull and cast turret were proof only against rifle and light machine gun rounds. Design work on what became the M8 began in June of 1942, with production beginning the following March. By the time Ford's St. Paul M8 assembly line was shut down in May 1945, 8,523 of these 6x6 vehicles had been built.

The Greyhound was armed with a 37mm M6 anti-tank gun mounted in its open topped turret. Mounted coaxial to the main gun was an M1919A4 .30-caliber machine gun. Antiaircraft defense was provided by a .50-caliber M2 HB machine gun installed on the turret. At first, an M49 ring with associated trolley and cradle was used for this installation, although on later models a machine gun socket was installed in the rear of the turret instead.

The clutch and accelerator controls of the M8 are hydraulic assisted.

The U.S. military phased the M8 out of service shortly after the Korean War, but the French used the cars as late as Vietnam.

Weight:	14,500 pounds
Size (LxWxH):	197" x 100" x 90"
Max Speed:	56 mph
Range:	250 miles

Patton Museum, Fort Knox, Ky.

Condition code	6	5	4	3	2	1	Scarcity
Value (dollars)	1,500	2,500	4,000	9,000	18,000	25,000	4

M20 Armored Utility Car

The M20, like the M8, was a six-wheeled armored car built by Ford at its St. Paul plant. Production began in July 1943 and, by the time the line closed down in June 1945, 3,791 of these high-speed utility vehicles had been produced. The M20 was also designed to be used as an armored transport for field commanders. Unlike its brother the M8, the M20 had no turret, rather was an open-topped vehicle. A .50-caliber M2 HB machine gun for defense against aircraft or infantry was mounted via a trolley and cradle to a ring mount attached to the top of the hull. Those units built prior to August 1944 were equipped with the ring mount M49, while those built after that date had the improved mount M66. Just like the M8, the mine racks of the early

M20s were replaced by large storage lockers during the course of the production run.

Communications was important in the reconnaissance role, and the M20 was normally equipped with one of the following sets: (SCR-506 or SCR-694C or AN/GRC-9) and (SCR-506 or SCR-608 or SCR-510 or SCR-619 or SCR-610); or (AN/VRC-3); or (AN/VRC-3); or (AN/GRC-3,-4,-5,-6,-7, or –8) and (SCR-506).

◆

Weight:	12,250 pounds
Size (LxWxH):	197" x 100" x 91"
Max Speed:	56 mph
Range:	250 miles

◆

Condition code	6	5	4	3	2	1	Scarcity
Value (dollars)	20,000	25,000	35,000	45,000	60,000	75,000	3

V-100/M706 Commando

Photos of the Cadillac Gage V-100 most often show the vehicle on convoy escort duty in Vietnam. However, a more common, albeit less glamorous, role was that of base security vehicle.

First tested in June 1962, the Cadillac Gage V-100 used many components "borrowed" from other military vehicles. The Chrysler 361 V-8 that powered it was also used in the M113. The axles beneath this armored 4x4 were similar to the axles used on M35 cargo trucks, with the addition of locking differentials.

The 14.00-20 tires, however, were of a special type, with special tread and of a run-flat design. "Commando" was even molded into the sidewalls of the tires. A 10,000-pound capacity hydraulically operated winch was mounted internally at the front of the vehicle. The fenders on the pilot models were cut out in an angular manner, whereas later vehicles had rounded fenders. There was no provision for deepwater fording because the vehicles were completely amphibious without preparation.

The turret could mount various combinations of machine guns, such as a pair of .30-caliber guns, or one .30 and one .50 caliber, or 7.62mm machine guns instead of the .30s.

Known to the Air Force as the V-100, but standardized by the Army as the M706, the production vehicles differed in detail from the XM706. One vision block and firing port on each side was deleted, and the roof hatches for the driver were raised slightly above the surface of the hull.

US Army TACOM LCMC

LAV Piranha

As threats to world peace become increasingly sophisticated, the complexity of countermeasures must increase as well. As a result, oftentimes multinational cooperation is required. The LAV Piranha is a prime example of such globalization. Designed by Motorwagenfabrik AG (MOWAG) of Switzerland, the LAV is built by General Motors of Canada.

Although the Army had expressed some interest in the vehicle in the 1970s, ultimately the Army decided against the LAV. However, the U.S. Marine Corps was keenly interested and began purchasing the LAV-25 in 1982. Ironically, during Operation Desert Storm, the Army's 82nd Airborne borrowed 15 LAVs from the Marine Corps.

Completely amphibious, the LAV is powered by the Detroit Diesel 6V53T diesel engine. On land, driver-selectable four- or eight-wheel drive can push the 12-ton vehicle up to 60 MPH. In the water, two rear propellers can push it up to 6 MPH.

The basic vehicle, the LAV-25, is armed with the 25mm M242 gun.

The LAV-C2 is a battalion command and control vehicle, and lacks a turret.

The LAV-M is a mortar carrier, armed with an 81mm M252 mortar.

The TOW missile carrier in this series is the LAV-AT, which has a two-tube missile launcher turret.

The LAV-R is the recovery variant, and has a 30,000-pound drag winch and a 6,600-pound capacity hydraulic crane.

The truck version, known as a Logistics Vehicle, is the LAV-L.

Twelve electronic warfare vehicles were built, which are designated MEWSS, Mobile Electronic Warfare Support System.

The LAV-AD air defense vehicles are armed with a 25mm GAU-12 Bushmaster Gatling gun and two quadruple Stinger missile launchers.

M93A1 Fox

With the threats on today's battlefield far more subtle than lead bullets flying through the air, new defensive technologies have also appeared in the military arena. One of the most sophisticated is the M93A1 Fox nuclear, biological, chemical reconnaissance vehicle. Developed by the Germans for their army, where it is known as the Fuchs, the vehicle came to the attention of U.S. forces in the 1980s.

Inside the Fox is a mass spectrometer that analyzes samples of air and soil for the presence of chemical and biological agents. Whereas the M93 had a four-man crew, the M93A1 has improved detection equipment, is highly automated and requires only a crew of three.

The M93A1 contains an enhanced NBC sensor suite consisting of the M21 Remote Sensing Chemical Agent Alarm (RSCAAL), MM1 Mobile Mass Spectrometer, Chemical Agent Monitor/Improved Chemical Agent Monitor (CAM/ICAM), AN/VDR-2 Beta Radiac and M22 Automatic Chemical Agent Detector/Alarm (ACADA). The NBC sensor suite has been digitally linked with the communications and navigation subsystems by a dual-purpose central processor system known as the Multipurpose Integrated Chemical Agent Detector (MICAD). The MICAD processor fully automates NBC warning and reporting functions. The M93A1 Fox is also equipped with an advanced Global Positioning System and the Autonomous Navigation System (ANAV) that enables the system to accurately locate and report agent contamination.

The M93A1 is built by General Dynamics Land Systems, while the M93 was built by Henschel Wehrtechnik, Kassel, Germany.

◆

Weight:	39,200 pounds
Size (LxWxH):	286.8" x 117.6" x 104.4"
Max Speed:	65 mph
Range:	510 miles

◆

Spc. John S. Gartler, U.S. Army

Stryker

Named for two Medal of Honor recipients, the Stryker is the centerpiece vehicle for the Army's Interim Brigade Combat Teams (IBCTs). The Stryker is a family of 10 19-ton wheeled armored vehicles based on the LAVIII design. Intended to be rapidly deployed by C-130 aircraft, the vehicle rolls off the aircraft combat-ready. Variations of the Stryker family include the Infantry Carrier Vehicle, Mobile Gun System, Anti-Tank Guided Missile Vehicle, Mortar Carrier Vehicle, Reconnaissance Vehicle, Fire Support Vehicle, Engineer Squad Vehicle, Commander's Vehicle, Medical Evacuation Vehicle, and a Nuclear, Biological and Chemical (NBC) Reconnaissance Vehicle. The vehicles have robust armor protection, can sustain speeds of 60 mph, and have self-recovery abilities and also have a central tire inflation system. The Infantry Carrier

Vehicle carries a nine-man infantry squad and a crew of two and has a Remote Weapon Station with an M2 .50-caliber machine gun or MK19, 40mm grenade launcher.

One of the earliest combat uses of the Stryker armored wheeled vehicles was a search for criminals and weapons as part of Operation Block Party in Mosul, Iraq, on Oct. 4, 2004. The 1st Battalion, 14th Cavalry Regiment, 3rd Brigade, Stryker Brigade Combat Team, 2nd Infantry Division, from Fort Lewis, Wash., was the unit involved.

◆

Weight:	36,240 pounds
Size (LxWxH):	275" x 107" x 104"
Max Speed:	62 mph
Range:	312 miles

◆

Section 2 Tracked Vehicles
Light Tanks

Library of Congress

Condition code	6	5	4	3	2	1	Scarcity
Value (dollars)	15,000	20,000	25,000	30,000	35,000	45,000	4

Tracked Vehicles

M3 Series Light Tanks

The standard family of light tanks of the U.S. Army at the outbreak of World War II was the M3, which had entered production at American Car and Foundry during March 1941. The M3, as well as the later M5, was listed as a G-103 vehicle, however, the M8 Howitzer Motor Carriage was listed as G-127.

These tanks, powered by the Continental W-670 radial engine, were produced until October 1942. In addition to these 4,526 tanks, there were 1,285 more built powered by the Guiberson T-1020. Rather than the usual "A" suffix, these diesel-powered tanks were designated "M3 light tank (diesel)."

Three different turrets were mounted on the M3s. The original turret was riveted, and the 279 intermediate turrets were welded faced hardened armor, where the final was welded homogeneous armor. Interestingly, in addition to the turret rotation, the main gun had a plus or minus 20 degrees traverse within its mount. Some of the later turrets did not have a cupola. The first 3,212 tanks were produced with riveted hulls; subsequent ones were assembled by welding.

◆

Weight:	28,000 pounds
Size (LxWxH):	178.4" x 88" x 104"
Max Speed:	36 mph
Armament:	37mm cannon, multiple machine guns

◆

14th Armored Recreations

Condition code	6	5	4	3	2	1	Scarcity
Value (dollars)	20,000	25,000	35,000	45,000	60,000	75,000	3

M5 Series Light Tanks

The M5 family was developed to provide the Army with a light tank that did not use a radial aircraft type engine, as did the M3 family. Cadillac converted an M3 by installing twin Cadillac engines and Hydramatic transmissions that drove the tank through a two-speed automatic transfer case.

The new power plant, as well as improved hull shape, gave the M5 much more interior space than that of the M3. Production of the M5 began at GM Cadillac Division's Detroit plant in April 1942. In August, production was also begun in Southgate, Calif. Massey Harris had begun building the M5 in July. M5 production ceased at all three facilities in December 1942, with the total run of 2,074.

The M5A1 was an improvement, featuring an enlarged turret similar to the one developed for the M3A3. The M5A1 replaced the M5 on the production lines at all three of the plants. Additional production was added by bringing American Car and

Foundry into the M5A1 manufacturing group. Production was completed at all four facilities by mid-1944, and totaled 6,810 of these improved light tanks.

Early models had the .30-caliber anti-aircraft machine gun exposed on the turret side, while later models incorporated a shield that the weapon retracted into.

Identifying early and late production of the M5A1 is made more difficult due to an extensive rebuilding program. Between November 1944 and June 1945 American Car and Foundry remanufactured 775 of the early models to the late model standards.

◆

Weight:	34,700 pounds
Size (LxWxH):	196" x 90" x 101"
Max Speed:	36 mph
Armament:	37mm cannon, three .30-caliber machine guns

◆

Pat Stansell

Condition code	6	5	4	3	2	1	Scarcity
Value (dollars)	15,000	25,000	35,000	48,000	60,000	68,000	4

M24 Chaffee Tank

The tanks in the U.S. arsenal at the outset of World War II were designed around the doctrine that the tank's role was to support infantry. Tanks were to be destroyed not by other tanks, but by specialized tank destroyers. Limitations were placed on the designs accordingly, with further limitations brought about by the engineering know-how and production facilities at hand.

American tanks tended to be tall and slab-sided, using volute suspension and aircraft engines. Self-propelled artillery (gun motor carriages) was in its infancy, with virtually all heavy artillery being towed. Even before the U.S. entry in the war, the combat experience of the British using U.S. tanks against German equipment was pointing toward the need for new designs, with bigger guns, improved armor and increased mobility.

The M24 light tank and the T26E3 (later redesignated M26) tank both used torsion bar suspension, affording a more stable gun platform and smoother ride. Both were designed around V-8 power, providing a lower profile, and both were constructed using welding and casting techniques, dispensing with the rivets that covered many earlier designs.

The M24, with its 75mm gun, was designed, produced and deployed fairly smoothly and rapidly as a direct replacement for the previously employed M5A1, which was armed with a 37mm gun. It was dubbed the Chaffee, for General Adna Chaffee.

◆

Weight:	40,500 pounds
Size (LxWxH):	216" x 117" x 97.5"
Max Speed:	34 mph
Armament:	75mm cannon, two .30-, one .50-caliber machine guns

◆

Patton Museum, Ft. Knox, Ky.

M551 Sheridan Tank

The M551 Sheridan is immediately recognized for its role in Vietnam. Less publicized was its successful use during Desert Storm. Designed to be a light reconnaissance tank, the M551 combined amphibious and airborne assault capabilities with a powerful main gun.

The 152mm Gun/Launcher could fire either conventional ammunition or the Shillelagh anti-tank missile. As the vehicle was designed primarily as a missile launcher, when firing conventional munitions the recoil of the big gun was tremendous, lifting the front of the lightweight vehicle from the ground.

Although the turret, usually the easiest target for enemy gunners, was made of conventional steel armor, the Sheridan's hull was made of welded 7039 aluminum alloy armor plate. This was done to keep the vehicle's weight low in conjunction with its role in airborne and amphibious assaults. The basic hull was enclosed in high-density foam to improve flotation and a second layer of aluminum was added all around to form the exterior surfaces.

During their service, the M551s had updated gun-laying systems installed. These vehicles were then classified M551A1.

The Allison Division of General Motors built 1,562 of these tanks beginning in 1966. Withdrawn from front-line services without a replacement after Desert Storm, some are in use at the desert training center masquerading as Soviet vehicles.

◆

Weight:	33,460 pounds
Size (LxWxH):	248.3" x 110" x 150"
Max Speed:	45 mph
Armament:	152mm Gun/Launcher, one .30-, one .50-caliber machine guns

◆

Medium Tanks

Library of Congress

M3 Lee Tank

The M3 series had its roots in the Ordnance Department's efforts in the late 1930s to develop a medium tank. By 1939, the M2 had been standardized and put into production at Rock Island Arsenal with a high velocity 37mm gun installed in a revolving turret.

However, battlefield reports from Europe indicated that the 37mm was no longer an adequate main gun. The newly established Armored Force stated that a 75mm gun would be required for the Army's medium tank. Two criteria led to the tank as we know it. First, the Rock Island Arsenal engineers were allotted only 60 days to design the new vehicle. This meant that the engineers set to work to produce an up-armored, up-gunned tank using the M2A1 as basis rather than a totally new design. Secondly, a turret ring that would handle such a large (for the time) weapon did not exist then in the U.S. and there was not enough time to develop one. The result was the unusual design of the M3 medium tanks with their 75mm main gun being mounted in a sponson on the right front of the hull.

From the outset, the M3 was considered an interim design. The Ordnance Committee in 1940 recognized the major drawback of the sponson-mounted main gun, and included a statement that "the next step in this development would consist of relocating the 75mm gun in the turret–this tank to be put into production as soon as it is determined that the changes are satisfactory." Originally, production of the interim M3 was to be limited to a few hundred units. However, facing the necessity of equipping the rapidly expanding U.S. Army as well as a devastated British armored force, it was decided to put the M3 into mass production. Ultimately it was superceded by the M4 Sherman, and the M3 series vehicles were classified as obsolete by 1945.

◆

Weight:	61,500 pounds
Size (LxWxH):	222" x 107" x 123"
Max Speed:	24 mph
Armament:	one 75mm cannon, one 37 mm cannon, three .30-caliber machine guns.

◆

Too few survivors of this type exist in private hands to establish values.

Patton Museum, Ft. Knox, Ky.

M4 Sherman Tank

The Sherman tank is remembered as the tank that won World War II for the United States and its allies. Even now, decades after the war, "Sherman Tank" is an instantly recognizable term with the general public. But the term "Sherman" tank describes not one type of vehicle, but several distinctive variations.

The M4 Sherman replaced the M3 Lee Sherman, with which it shared many parts, on the assembly lines. Chief among the carried-over components was its powerplant. Compact size and lightweight powerplants were then, and still are, of great interest to tank designers. It is no surprise that the powerplants of many early U.S. tanks, including the M3 and M4 medium tanks, were based on aircraft engines (the technology of the turbine engine of today's M1 Abrams is based on that of a turbojet aircraft engine, so the pattern continues). The nine-cylinder air-cooled radial engine originally used in the M3 and M4 was an adaptation of the R975 Wright Whirlwind engine that powered many U.S. aircraft during World War II.

Use of this engine had a two-fold effect on the Sherman. First, the large diameter of the radial caused the tank's hull to be comparatively tall (and thus a larger target). Secondly, the huge demand for the powerplant by the aircraft industry hastened the search for alternate powerplants.

Pat Stansell

M4A1(76)W Sherman Tank

The 75mm gun with which the M4 series was armed was found to be ineffective against a number of the tanks they encountered in Europe. The most expedient means of up-arming the Sherman was by using a 76mm gun mounted in a turret modified from the medium tank T23. The T23 itself was never standardized, nor did it see combat. The first M4A1(76)Ws had a split hatch for the loader, but in time that was replaced with the small oval hatch.

Ammunition explosions, set off by damage that would not otherwise disable the tank, were fatal to the crews and demoralizing to their comrades. Hence, wet ammunition stowage was devised. Double-walled ammunition lockers were devised, with the space between the walls filled with a water/antifreeze mixture. In the event these ammunition boxes were breached, the water would prevent an ammunition fire. The wet ammunition stowage, coupled with the relocated ammunition racks, greatly reduced the number of casualties. Tanks with wet ammunition storage are denoted by a (W) in the model number.

The M4A1 differed from other Sherman models in having a cast steel, rather than fabricated, hull. Lima Locomotive Works, Lima, Ohio, began producing the cast-hulled M4A1 in February 1942, and Pressed Steel Car Company began production the next month. Pacific Car and Foundry began producing the M4A1 in May 1942. Lima built its last M4A1 with 75mm gun in September 1943, Pacific in November and Pressed Steel stopped in December. The three plants' production totaled 6,281 tanks. The Pressed Steel Car Co. converted to the M4A1(76) production in January 1944. By the time the war ended, it had built 3,426 of these machines.

Patton Museum, Ft. Knox, Ky.

M4A3 Sherman Tank

The variant of the Sherman that came to be "America's tank" was the M4A3. The search for an alternate powerplant brought about a model designation change. However, the "alternate" engine came to be viewed not as a substitute, but as a preferred improvement. The engine installed in the M4A3 was the Ford-designed and -built model GAA V-8 liquid-cooled gasoline engine. Again, the aeronautical connection is present, as the GAA was an adaptation of an experimental Ford V-12 aircraft engine.

Because of the similarities of the chassis, an M3 medium tank was modified for testing of the new engine, the tank then being redesignated M3E1. The engine passed its tests with flying colors, noted for its small size, high horsepower rating and ease of maintenance.

Ford began production of the M4A3 in May 1942, although Ford's production of the tank would be relatively short lived. (Ford M4A3 production ended in September 1943.) M4A3 and variant production was continued by Fisher Tank Arsenal and Chrysler's Detroit Tank Arsenal until eventually reaching a total of 12,596 units.

The slab-sided, V-8 powered M4A3 Sherman would form the backbone of America's armored force throughout World War II and well into the next decade. Like the other models of the Sherman, it would be the basis for an assortment of variants during the course of the war and after.

M4A3 76(W) Sherman Tank

Four different versions of 76mm guns were used in the T23 turrets on the various models of Sherman. The first was the 76mm Gun M1, followed by the M1A1, which had the outside recoil surface lengthened by one foot. This allowed the trunnions to be moved forward, better balancing the gun. The M1A1C had the end of the barrel threaded to permit installation of a muzzle brake, which sometimes wasn't fitted. The final version, the M1A2, was rifled one turn in 32 calibers rather than the one turn in 40 of the other 76mm guns. Muzzle brakes were installed on all M1A2 guns.

General data on various Sherman models:

Model	M4	M4A1	M4A2	M4A3	M4A3(76)	M4A4
Weight^	66,900	66,800	70,200	66,700	74,200	69,700
Length*	232	230	233	232.5	297	238.5
Width*	103	103	103	103	118	103
Height*	108	108	108	108	117	108
Crew	5	5	5	5	5	5
Max speed	24	24	25	26	26	25
Fuel capy	175	175	148	168	168	160
Range	120	120	150	130	100	100
Armament main	75MM	75MM	75MM	75MM	76MM	75MM
Secondary	1 X .50	1 X .50	1 X .50	1 X .50	1 X .50	1 X .50
Flexible	2 X .30	2 X .30	2 X .30	2 X .30	2 X .30	2 X .30

^ Fighting weight
*Overall dimensions listed in inches.

Engines installed in various model Shermans:

Engine make/model	Continental R975 C3	GM 6046	Chrysler A57
Number of cylinders	9	2 X 6	30
Displacement	973	850	1253
Horsepower	400 @ 2400 RPM	410 @ 2100	425 @ 2400 RPM
Torque	890 @ 1800 RPM	885 @ 1900	1060 @ 1800 RPM

M4A3E8 Sherman Tank

Trial vehicles with upgraded Horizontal Volute Suspension System (HVSS-discussed later), wet ammunition stowage and uparmed with a 76mm gun were known as M4A3E8 tanks. When this became standardized, the official nomenclature designated these vehicles as M4A3(76)W HVSS, but the name Easy Eight (as in M4A3E8) stuck, and the tanks are so known to this day.

During the course of the war, the Sherman was the platform of choice for many specialized vehicles, flamethrowers, bridge launchers, rocket launchers, etc. The following photos however showcase only the primary variants of Sherman gun tanks.

Condition code	6	5	4	3	2	1	Rarity
Value (dollars)	30,000	40,000	60,000	70,000	85,000	95,000	5

T26E3/M26/M46 Pershing Tank

For most of World War II, American tanks tended to be tall and slab-sided, using volute suspension and aircraft engines. Even before the U.S. entry in the war, the combat experience of the British using U.S. tanks against German equipment was pointing toward the need for new designs, with bigger guns, improved armor and increased mobility. However, improvements were slow in coming due largely to inter-agency bickering within the Army about armor, armament and propulsion.

Delays occurred not only in the design stage, but even after the new tank, designated at the time T26E3 (later M26), entered production there were numerous delays getting the new tank to the field. Only after threats to carry the matter to General Marshall was it decided to deploy 20 tanks to Europe as part of the Zebra Mission. The intent of this mission was to provide testing of weapons for a postwar Army in combat conditions.

The Pershing used torsion bar suspension, affording a stable gun platform and smooth ride. It had Ford V-8 power, providing a low profile, and was constructed using welding and casting, eliminating the rivets that covered many earlier designs.

The new tank was such a success that production continued at both Chrysler's Detroit Tank Arsenal and at the GM's Grand Blanc Tank Arsenal for two years after VJ Day. At the same time, almost every other defense contract was terminated. Many of these tanks proved themselves in Korea, facing down Soviet-built T-34s.

The Pershing's weak link was its engine. The 41-ton tank was more than the 500 horsepower Ford-built GAF engine could handle. To correct this deficiency, most of the M26 tanks were upgraded to M46s with an improved engine and other changes during the Korean War and for a period afterward. The "Heavy" tank designation was officially changed to "Medium Tank" after the war in 1946.

Weight: 92,000 pounds
Size (LxWxH): 333.625" x 137" x 109"
Max Speed: 30 mph
Armament: 90mm gun M3, two .30-, one .50-caliber machine guns

Verne Kindischi

Condition code	6	5	4	3	2	1	Rarity
Value (dollars)	30,000	40,000	60,000	66,000	80,000	90,000	5

M47 Tank

The outbreak of the war in Korea raised serious concerns that World War III was at hand. America's leadership rushed many vehicles into production in preparation for that possibility. One such vehicle was the M47 Medium Tank. Though it entered production in April 1951, it was completed too late for the Korean War.

Essentially the design combined the one-piece cast turret of the experimental T42 with the M46 hull. The new turret mounted a 90mm main gun, and its armor is from two to four inches thick. Like the M46, the M47 was powered by a gasoline engine, a Continental AV-1790-5B, 12 cylinders, 820 horsepower, gasoline-propelled engine. The big Continental was thirsty and the range was meager.

Quick identifying features of the M-47 are the sharply tapered turret with small gun shield and unusually long narrow turret bustle. Initially a .50-caliber Browning machine gun was mounted co-axial with the 90mm gun. Later production had a .30-caliber Browning machine gun mounted instead. Also on early models, an M2 HB .50-caliber Browning machine gun was mounted via a rotating ring to the commander's hatch, but this too was changed, being replaced by a fixed pintle mount for the big Browning.

The Chrysler-managed Detroit Arsenal built 3,443 M47 tanks between 1952 and 1954, and American Locomotive Co. built a similar number. Some of these tanks used hulls salvaged from M46 tanks while others had new hulls fabricated for them.

◆

Weight: 101,775 pounds
Size (LxWxH): 335" x 138.25" x 116 5/16"
Max speed: 30 mph
Armament: 90mm gun M36, two .30-, one .50-caliber machine guns

◆

Don F. Pratt Museum, Ft. Campbell, Ky.

Condition code	6	5	4	3	2	1	Rarity
Value (dollars)	30,000	40,000	60,000	66,000	80,000	90,000	5

M48A2 Patton Tank

The M48 was an outgrowth of M26/46 Pershing series of tanks, with the M47 as a stopgap until the new M48, initially the T48, could be fully developed. The M48 was produced in a variety of models. The most noteworthy of these is the M48A2, which was America's main tank in Vietnam.

The M48A2 introduced a fuel-injected engine to the series, which notably increased the range. The new power pack had relocated oil coolers, which increased space available in the engine compartment space and allowed larger fuel tanks on either side. This also brought about an improved engine deck of the M48A2 design to accommodate these changes. The new design eliminated the majority of the tank's infrared signature. The exhaust was no longer directed out the top of the rear deck, but instead was routed through two large louvered doors at the rear of the hull. This rear armor

design remained basically unchanged through the rest of this series, as well as the M60 Patton series. Most M48A2s have three return rollers rather than the five per each side on earlier models. An exception appears to be Marine Corps vehicles, which evidently kept the five-roller system.

The M48A2 and its subtypes were produced in greater abundance than any of the others, and remained in production until 1959. A later variation of the M48A2 was known as the M48A2C. The M48A2C had a coincidence range finder rather than the troublesome stereoscopic range finder of earlier models.

◆

Weight: 105,000 pounds
Size (LxWxH): 342" x 143.5" x 121.875"
Max Speed: 30 mph
Armament: 90mm gun M41, one .30-, one .50-caliber machine guns

◆

US Army TACOM LCMC

U.S. Military Vehicles Field Guide

M60 Patton Tank

Development of the M60 series of tanks began in response to the Soviet T-54. The new M60 was patterned along the lines of the very successful M48 series, the major improvement being the adoption of an Americanized version of the British L7 105mm cannon, known as the M68 semi-automatic 105mm gun.

The first M60 entered production at the Chrysler-managed Detroit Tank Arsenal in 1960. Only 2,205 of the original M60s were built before being superceded by the M60A1.

The only crewman housed in the hull of the M60, which was made from five large steel castings that have been welded together, was the driver. As with most modern U.S. tanks, the balance of the crew of four rode in the turret; a gunner to the right, the commander directly behind him and the loader on the left of the 105mm gun. All the tanks of the M60 series used a 12-cylinder Continental diesel engine. This engine is a fuel-injected and turbosupercharged 90-degree V-12.

The M60 was not used in Vietnam, although some support variants were, such as bridge launchers and engineer vehicles.

Weight:	102,000 pounds
Size (LxWxH):	366.5" x 141" x 126.34"
Max Speed:	30 mph
Armament:	105mm gun M68, one .30-, one .50-caliber machine guns

Main Battle Tanks

Patton Museum, Ft. Knox, Ky.

M103 Heavy Tank

When the Korean War broke out, concerns arose it would escalate into a clash of superpowers and the U.S. did not have an equal to Russia's heavy tank. Work began in earnest on what was to become the M103. Only 300 were ultimately built, all at Chrysler's Newark, Del., tank plant. Plagued with flaws, the tank was not perfected until the Korean War was over.

Eighty had been produced when problems began to be discovered. These were stored as corrections were sought. Ultimately, almost 100 changes were made. As modified, the tank was standardized as M103 in April 1956 and the balance of the order filled.

Despite these improvements, the tank fell short of expectations and no more were ordered. Rejected by the Army, the M103 found favor with the Marines, who used the behemoth, with further updates, for 30 years.

The M103 was armed with a 120mm gun, flanked by .30-caliber coaxial machine guns. A remote control .50-caliber machine gun was mounted in the commander's cupola.

The M103 was the heaviest and most heavily armed tank fielded by the U.S. until the Abrams appeared 35 years later.

Using the same Continental AV-1790-5C 12 cylinder, 1791 cid gas engine found in the much smaller M47 medium tank, even with 810 horsepower, the M103 was underpowered.

The T43/M103 resembles an oversized M48 due to its similarly shaped, but much larger, hull.

◆

Weight:	126,000 pounds
Size (Lxwxh):	445.5" x 148" x 113.38"
Max speed:	25mph
Range:	80 miles
Main gun:	120mm
Secondary:	two .30-, one .50-caliber machine guns

Only one M103 is known to be in private hands.

◆

M1, M1A1 Abrams Tank

Despite having a troubled and controversial testing period and initial deployment, the Abrams, shown here in M1A1 form, has proven its ability to dominate the battlefield. Named in honor Gen. Creighton W. Abrams, former Army chief of staff and proponent of the advanced armored crew protection, the M1 family has arguably the most advanced ground fighting vehicles on the planet.

Chobham spaced armor (ceramic blocks set in resin between layers of conventional armor) protects the crew and the vehicle against most conventional and advanced munitions. In addition to the armor, the Abram's crew is also protected by the layout of its ammunition stowage, with the majority of the main gun ammunition in the turret bustle behind a bulkhead. In the event of an ammunition explosion, blowoff panels in the turret bustle's roof would vent the explosion out of the tank while the bulkhead doors protected the crew from danger. During operation, the ammunition is reached through fast-closing access doors; the operation time for these doors is 250 milliseconds.

The powerful gas turbine powerplant, while having high fuel consumption, adds high speed to the Abrams' defenses. Its Rhinemetall 120mm main gun is equipped with a sophisticated fire control system, providing stabilization for accurate shooting on the move. Thermal-imaging night sights allow around-the-clock accurate fire, especially when combined with the Abrams' laser range finder and digital ballistic computer.

The M1A1, which entered production in 1985, features a different turret than that of the previously built, 105mm armed, M1.

Weight:	136,800 pounds
Size (Lxwxh):	388" x 144" x 96"
Max Speed:	41.5 mph
Range:	275 miles
Main Gun:	120mm
Secondary:	two 7.62mm, one .50-caliber machine guns

Third Cavalry Museum, Ft. Carson, Colo.

M1A2 Abrams Tank

In addition to all the M1A1 features, the latest Abrams, the M1A2, has a commander's independent thermal viewer, position navigation equipment and a digital data bus and radio interface unit providing a common picture among M1A2s on the battlefield. Approximately 1,000 of the older M1 tanks were rebuilt to the M1A2 configuration, which involved, among other things, installing an all-new turret.

Currently, the M1A2 System Enhancement Program (SEP) is adding second-generation thermal sensors and a thermal management system to the vehicle's electronics. The SEP includes upgrades to processors/memory that enable the M1A2 to use the Army's common command and control software, enabling the rapid transfer of digital situational data and overlays.

It is powered by a 1,500-horsepower Textron Lycoming AGT engine, delivering 3,800 torque.

◆

Weight:	139,000 pounds
Size (LxWxH):	388" x 144" x 96"
Max Speed:	42 mph
Range:	265 miles
Main Gun:	120mm
Secondary:	two 7.62mm, one .50-caliber machine guns

◆

Armored Personnel Carriers

US Army TACOM LCMC

Condition code	6	5	4	3	2	1	Rarity
Value (dollars)	2,000	5,000	8,000	12,000	16,000	21,000	4

M59 Armored Personnel Carrier

The M75 gave the Army most of what it was asking for in a personnel carrier. However, it was an expensive vehicle, which limited the number that could be purchased. Accordingly, a less expensive alternative was sought. The result was the M59, which not only was less expensive, but incorporated a number of other improvements. Chief of these was its rear ramp that lowered, allowing quick loading and unloading; even a Jeep could be driven inside. A small personnel door installed in the rear ramp allowed the crew to enter or exit.

Rather than the single large tank engine and cross drive transmission of the M75, the M59 used a pair of GMC 302 straight-six engines and 300MG Hydramatic transmissions similar to those used in the GMC M135 6x6 trucks. In emergency situations, the M59 could operate on a single engine, but it was slow going, for even with both engines running the M59 was seriously underpowered.

Weight:	42,600 pounds
Size (LxWxH):	221" x 128.5" x 94"
Max Speed, land:	32 mph
Max Speed, water:	4.3 mph
Range, land:	120 miles

Condition code	6	5	4	3	2	1	Rarity
Value (dollars)	2,000	5,000	8,000	12,000	16,000	21,000	4

Verne Kindischi

M75 Armored Infantry Vehicle

Throughout World War II, American armored personnel carriers were open-topped vehicles. This exposed the troops inside to snipers, air-burst artillery, aerial gunfire and harsh weather. Even before the war was over, work began designing fully enclosed armored personnel carriers. The M75 was the first mass-produced vehicle that resulted from these studies. Produced too late for World War II, the M75 proved itself in combat in Korea in 1953. Unfortunately, with a cost of $72,000 each, it was too expensive to be procured in the huge quantities the Army wanted.

Both FMC and International Harvester built the M75, in two large groups. The powerplant of the M75 consisted of the 375 horsepower AO-895-4 Continental engine coupled to a CD-500 cross drive transmission. There were two doors on the rear of the vehicle for troops to use, while the commander had a roof-mounted cupola with a M2 HB machine gun and the driver had a hatch on the upper sloping armor.

By today's standards, the M75 was noticeably tall for an APC.

Weight:	41,500 pounds
Size (LxWxH):	204" x 112" x 119.75"
Max Speed:	44.5 mph
Range, land:	115 miles

US Army/TACOM LCMC

Condition code	6	5	4	3	2	1	Rarity
Value (dollars)	3,000	6,000	10,000	14,000	19,000	25,000	4

M113

The shape of this vehicle has become readily identifiable as the American armored personnel carrier. This is no doubt largely due to its, and its variants', long service life. The M113 has been the Army's standard APC since production began at FMC in 1960.

The hull of the M113 vehicles was made of aluminum armor. A hydraulically operated ramp in the rear allowed rapid loading and unloading of troops, while a personnel door mounted in the door allowed crew access. The driver's position was in the left front, and the power plant was to the driver's right. The driver was provided with four M17 periscopes and his hatch had provision for a M19 infrared periscope as well. The commander's station was behind the driver and powerplant, and he had a cupola equipped with five M17 periscopes and a M2 HB machine gun. There were provisions for 11 passengers to ride in the carrier. An unusual feature of the M113 was the hydraulically tensioned track, rather than the usual hand-adjusted track of other armored vehicles. The M113 was amphibious, being propelled in the water by its tracks. However, there was only 14 inches of freeboard when the vehicle was in the water.

A Chrysler 75M V-8 engine driving through an Allison TX200-2 engine powered the M113. There were 4,974 M113s built for the U.S. armed forces, and 9,839 supplied to other countries.

◆

Weight: 20,310 pounds
Size (LxWxH): 191.5" x 105.75" x 98.25"
Max Speed: 40 mph
Range, land: 200 miles

◆

US Army TACOM LCMC

Condition code	6	5	4	3	2	1	Rarity
Value (dollars)	3,000	6,000	10,000	14,000	19,000	25,000	4

M113A1

The ink was hardly dry on the initial production contracts for the M113 when work began on a diesel-powered version. After trials of various versions, a version powered by the General Motors 6V53 V-6 diesel engine was standardized as M113A1 in May 1963, with production beginning the following year. The V-6 diesel's power was transmitted to the track through an Allison TX-100 automatic transmission and a DS-200 controlled differential.

This version of the M113 was used extensively in Vietnam, where the VC dubbed it the "green dragon." It was in Vietnam that the concept of the Infantry Fighting Vehicle really began to come into its own. Having early on been provided with a few of these APC, the ARVN began to fight from the vehicle, rather than simply using it as a taxi. In addition to the commander's .50-caliber machine gun, troopers also fought from the top hatches in the cargo area. After 14 .50-caliber

gunners were lost at the battle of Ap Bac in January 1963, work began to provide some degree of armor protection for the exposed gun positions.

FMC designed a circular gun shield for the commander's .50-caliber, which could be added to his cupola. Additionally, shielded mounts for two 7.62mm M60 machine guns, one on either side of the rear hatch, were installed.

Vehicles so modified were referred to as the M-113 Armored Cavalry vehicle (ACAV). In addition to a driver and its commander, the ACAV was crewed by two M-60 gunners and two loaders. One of the loaders had an M-79 40mm grenade launcher.

◆

Weight: 21,474 pounds
Size (LxWxH): 191.5" x 105.75" x 98.25"
Max Speed: 37 mph
Range: 300 miles

◆

Third Cavalry Museum, Ft. Carson, Colo.

M113A2

Many GIs, like these, rode into battle in Iraq in an updated version of the venerable APC known at the M113A2.

Introduced in 1979, the M113A2 was a result of the ongoing quest for greater performance. Prominent among the changes was a new fuel system using identical dual armored tanks, visible here, mounted on either side of the door. The M113A2 had an improved suspension system and engine-cooling system, as well. The power train was upgraded with the addition of a turbosupercharger to the engine, and the replacement of the

TX-100 and DS-200 with an Allison X200-3 cross drive transmission. With the cross drive transmission, the steering levers of previous models were replaced with a steering wheel and brake pedal.

◆

Weight:	21,608 pounds
Size (LxWxH):	208.5" x 105.75" x 98.25"
Max Speed:	37 mph
Range:	300 miles
Currently in use	

◆

M113A3

The aluminum armor of the M113, which had been adequate in 1960, was in need of an upgrade 25 years later. This upgrade was found in the P-900 applique armor kit. The M113A3, introduced in 1987, was equipped for the installation of this kit, and offered additional improvements as well. The external fuel tanks, an option on the M113A2, became standard on the M113A3. The transmission was upgraded from the X200-3 to the X200-4 version as well.

◆

Weight: 23,575 pounds
Size (LxWxH): 208.5" x 105.75" x 98.25"
Max Speed: 41 mph
Range: 300 miles
Currently in use.

◆

M106 107mm Self-propelled Mortar

The M106 was essentially a M113 with a round roof hatch through which the rear-facing mortar fired. It was mounted below on a 90-degree traversing mechanism. The mortar, the 107mm M30, was originally classified as the 4.2" mortar M30, but was redesignated when the U.S. Army adopted the metric system.

Procurement of the Chrysler gas engine-powered M106 began even before the type had been standardized. Of the 860 units FMC built, 589 went to U.S. forces and the balance to overseas sales.

When production of the base M113 vehicles changed from gasoline engine-driven units to diesel-powered machines, so did the mortar carrier, becoming the M106A1. The U.S. military received 982

of these, with a further 334 provided for overseas sales. When the M113A1 was again upgraded, becoming the M113A2, the M106 followed suit, getting the same upgrades and becoming the M106A2.

A base plate for the mortar was stowed on the rear outer left side of the hull, allowing the weapon to be removed from the vehicle and fired.

M106A1
Weight: 26,000 pounds
Size (LxWxH): 194" x 112.75" x 98.25"
Max Speed: 37 mph
Range: 300 miles

US Army TACOM LCMC

M901 TOW Missile Launcher

In times past, destroying enemy tanks at long ranges required powerful, high-velocity guns, usually mounted on heavily armored vehicles. The TOW (Tube-launched, Optically-tracked, Wire-guided) missile changed that. Its hollow-charge warhead, rocket motor and wire-guided accuracy, light weight and small size opened many new possibilities. It was natural that the lightweight M113 family was the basis for a carrier for this weapon system. Emerson Electric Co. developed the vehicle that became the M901. Known as the Hammerhead, there were 10 TOW missiles stored in the hull and two more transported in the launcher itself.

When upgraded to accommodate the TOW 2 and TOW 2A missiles, the classification was changed to M901A1. When the RISE power pack was installed, the vehicle became M901A3.

◆

M901A1
Weight: 26,000 pounds
Size (LxWxH): 191.5" x 112.75" x 134.25"
Max Speed: 40 mph
Range: 300 miles

◆

M981 Fire Support Team Vehicle (FIST-V)

The Fire Support Team Vehicle (FIST-V) is designed to provide an artillery forward observer to mechanized infantry as well armor units. It serves chiefly to provide FIST HQ with an operating base for targeting, self-locating and designating equipment. This leads to greater first round accuracy, and mobility and survivability for the artillery observers comparable with the maneuver units being supported.

Based on the M113A2, the FIST-V incorporated many components of the M901. Its G/VLLD (ground/vehicle laser locator designator) turret is designed to resemble the Emerson Electric TOW missile launcher of the M901 in an effort to camouflage the vehicle. This design also allows the vehicle's crew to work from hull-down positions. However, the M981 is only armed with a 7.62mm machine gun in the commander's cupola. With the RISE power pack installed, the M981 is known as the M981A2.

The FIST-V has secure voice and digital communication capability.

A north-seeking gyrocompass and night sight are aboard the FIST-V

M981A1
Weight: 27,900 pounds
Size (LxWxH): 208.5" x 105.75" x 134.25"
Max Speed: 40 mph
Range: 300 miles

Condition code	6	5	4	3	2	1	Rarity
Value (dollars)	3,000	6,000	8,500	12,000	17,000	22,000	3

Armored Command and Reconnaissance Carrier

Though the M114 somewhat resembles the M113, the 114 is not an armored personnel carrier at all. Rather, its intended role was more closely aligned with that of the World War II-era M3A1 and M8 armored cars–to probe for enemy forces, radio their position and beat a hasty retreat once contact was made.

Unfortunately, its off-road performance was not adequate to this task. Particularly deplorable was the fact that the hull extended forward of the tracks, causing the bow to dig in when crossing obstacles, immobilizing the carrier.

The Cadillac-built vehicle was fully amphibious and air-transportable. Water propulsion was provided by its shrouded tracks. With its low profile, there was only space for the three-man crew of driver, commander, observer and a single passenger inside the M114. Power was provided by a Chevy 283 V-8 engine and Hydramatic transmission. It rode on torsion bar suspension.

On early models, the commander had a cupola with an externally mounted .50 caliber machine gun, while on later models this was replaced by a turret-type arrangement. The observer had a hatch on the right side of the hull, just rear of the commander's position. The observer was provided with two pedestal mounts for his machine gun. A large circular door was in the rear wall of the hull.

The M114A1, the most numerous of the series, had a turret-type machine gun mount on the hull roof.

Production of the lightweight, aluminum-armored vehicle began in 1962 and the last variants were retired in the early 1980s.

Weight: 14,749 pounds
Size (LxWxH): 175.75" x 91.75" x 91.125"
Max Speed: 40 mph
Range: 300 miles

US Army TACOM LCMC

M2A2 Bradley

The only differences between the early M2 and M3 vehicles visible to the casual observer were the absence of side firing ports on the M3. Depending on the variant, six to seven infantry soldiers ride in the back of the M2 series vehicle.

The M2 series Bradley has a two-man turret housing a 25mm Bushmaster chain gun, with a 7.62mm M240C machine gun mounted coaxially. A two-tube TOW missile launcher is attached to the turret. Firing the TOW requires that the vehicle be brought to a stop. Two four-tube smoke grenade launchers are mounted on either side of the turret face. The GE Bushmaster 25mm chain gun can fire single shots, 100 or 200 rounds per minute, as selected by the gunner. Its dual feed mechanism allows the gunner to switch instantly to select either high explosive and armor-piercing ammunition.

The rear of the vehicle is a large loading ramp, which was fitted with an emergency door in the left side.

When the M2 was upgraded to fire the TOW2 missile, it was redesignated the M2A1. At the same time, a gas particulate NBC filtration system was added. The Cummins VTA-903 500-horsepower diesel engine powers the M2 and M2A1.

To counter increased threats, a more heavily armored version was created, the M2A2. Included on the M2A2 are also fittings that allow for the attachment of either passive or explosive reactive armor tiles. Liners in the body protect men from shell splinters. Many M2s and M2A1s were rebuilt to the M2A2 standard.

The engine was upgraded to handle the additional weight, now being a 600-horsepower Cummins VTA-903T engine.

The Bradley is amphibious after preparation.

Weight:	60,000 pounds
Size (LxWxH):	258" x 129" x 117"
Max Speed:	35 mph
Range:	250 miles

Third Cavalry Museum, Ft. Carson, Colo.

M3A2 Bradley

The M3 was basically the same vehicle as the M2, without firing ports and with a different interior arrangement. The M3 was built to be a cavalry scout vehicle for M1 Abrams-equipped armored formations. Instead of being filled with armed troops, its passenger compartment was occupied by two observers and a scout motorcycle. The M3 also carries 600 more rounds of ammunition for the Bushmaster and five more TOW missiles than the M2.

The M3-series received the same improvements as the M2-series, and when the M2A1 was fielded, so was the M3A1. Also, on the M3A1, four periscopes mounted in the cargo hatch proper replaced the three periscopes on the rear deck.

Once again, when the IFV was improved, so was the Cavalry Fighting Vehicle, becoming the M3A2. In addition to improved armor protection, the observers were repositioned to the left side of the vehicle's passenger compartment, and the missile stowage was relocated.

◆

Weight: 60,000 pounds
Size (LxWxH): 258" x 129" x 117"
Max Speed: 35 mph
Range: 250 miles

◆

US Army TACOM LCMC

M3A3 Bradley

After Operation Desert Storm, the M3A2 was upgraded based on lessons learned. The M3A3 is the most electronically sophisticated of the Bradley family. Among its electronic upgrades are the 1553 databus, central processing unit, and information displays for the vehicle commander and squad leader. These improvements made the M3A3 compatible with the intervehicular communication systems used by M1A2 Abrams tank and AH-64D Apache Longbow helicopter. The commander's station is equipped with an independent thermal viewer, as well as the Improved Bradley Acquisition System (IBAS).

The IBAS is a new integrated sight unit that allows automatic gun adjustments, automatic bore-sighting and tracking of dual targets. The CITV and integrated sight are both second-generation FLIR systems. The roof was reinforced with titanium armor. These vehicles were manufactured by rebuilding older M3A2 Bradleys.

◆

Weight: 61,000 pounds
Size (LxWxH): 258" x 129" x 117"
Max Speed: 35 mph
Range: 250 miles

◆

Tracked Vehicles

US Army TACOM LCMC

M270 MLRS

Built by Lockheed-Martin, the M270 looks nothing like the other members of the Bradley family. However, this vehicle and its three-man crew pack by far the heaviest punch of the series. Designed to provide counter-battery fire and suppress enemy defenses, it can engage targets at ranges from seven to 150 miles.

The chassis of the Bradley was lengthened to form the basis of the Multiple Launch Rocket System, becoming M993 Multiple Launch Rocket System carrier. Upon this chassis was mounted the M270 ground vehicle-mounted rocket launcher. The launcher housed two rocket pods that are each loaded with six 227mm M26 rockets. These rockets could be fired one at a time or in rapid sequence. Each M26 rocket carries 644 M77 submunitions.

◆

Weight:	54,500 pounds
Size (LxWxH)	274.5" x 117" x 102"
Max Speed:	40 mph
Range:	300 miles

◆

Tracked Vehicles

Amphibious Landing Vehicles

Condition code	6	5	4	3	2	1	Rarity
Value (dollars)	15,000	20,000	25,000	30,000	35,000	45,000	5

Tracked Vehicles

LVT(A)(5)

As Allied forces pushed ashore in the Pacific during World War II, they met fierce resistance. Troops, primarily Marines, were in desperate need for armored support from the moment they crawled ashore. Responding to this problem, a 37mm gun, mounted in a turret similar to that of the M3 light tank, was mounted on an amphibious tractor or LVT. This vehicle, which was also armored, was designated the LVT(A)(1).

While this vehicle proved the theory sound, practically speaking the 37mm gun simply was not large enough. Accordingly, a new turret, housing a 75mm howitzer,

was designed. When so equipped, the Alligator was given new nomenclature, LVT(A)(4). When an improved turret with power traverse and turret basket was added in April 1945, the vehicle was again redesignated, this time as LVT(A)(5).

◆

Weight:	40,000 pounds
Size (LxWxH):	319" x 128" x 122.5"
Max Speed, land:	15 mph
Max Speed, water:	7 mph
Main Weapon:	75mm
Engine:	Continental W670-9A radial

◆

LVTP5

The various LVT used during World War II proved the merit of Roebling's amphibious tractor, but also showed room for improvement. Notably, there was a desire to house the troops in a totally enclosed compartment to better protect them during landings. The LVTP5 addressed this concern, and additionally was much larger and had significantly better performance in water, largely the result of the hull front having an inverted-V shape.

Developed in 1951 by the Ingersoll Products Division of Borg-Warner, production began in August 1952. On previous Amtracs the tracks wrapped around the circumference of the hull, but the LVTP5 tracks were mounted low on the hull much like a tank. The inverted grousers on the tracks propelled the vehicle while it was in water. The upper run of track ran an internal return channel to prevent it from providing negative thrust.

The V-shaped bow of the LVTP5 could be lowered to form a ramp for loading and unloading cargo and carrying up to 34 infantry troops (25 for water operation). Additionally, three hatches over the passenger compartment provided alternate means of loading and unloading the vehicle. The crew and passenger compartment was at the front of the vehicle, with the driver's position at the front above the left track channel. The powerplant was located at the rear of the vehicle.

Famed sniper Carlos Hathcock was critically burned when a LVTP he was riding struck a mine in Vietnam.

Weight:	87,780 pounds
Size (LxWxH):	356" x 140.5" x 103"
Max Speed, land:	30 mph
Max Speed, water:	6.8 mph
Range, land:	190 miles

Sadly, though obsolete, this vehicle has not become available on the collector market

AAVP7A1

Originally designated the LVTP7A1, they were re-designated in 1984 by the Marine Corps as AAVP7A1. Since that time this vehicle has been notably visible in televised accounts of the Marine Corps operations in Iraq.

Marine operations in Vietnam showed some shortcomings in the LVTP5 design, and the LVTP7 was intended to overcome these problems. FMC completed the first prototype of the new vehicle during the summer of 1967, and issue to troops began in 1972.

Water jets on either side of the vehicle pushed the LVTP7 through the water, but perhaps even more importantly, troops exited this vehicle at the rear, eliminating a previously tempting, and often deadly, target for enemy gunners during amphibious landings. As a result of these changes, the LVTP7 had a completely new look.

The vehicle commander was armed with a M139 20mm gun and a coaxial 7.62 machine gun. Roof hatches allowed cargo to be loaded by crane, as well as cargo and men to enter while at sea.

In the early 1980s, a service life extension program (SLEP) began on the LVTP7. A Cummins VT400 diesel replaced the GM 8V53T engine originally used and the transmission was replaced as well. Many of the hydraulic systems were replaced with electrical, and the suspension and fuel systems improved. A new weapons station armed with both a .50 caliber machine gun and a 40mm automatic grenade launcher replaced the commander's weapons. FMC converted 853 of the old vehicles to the new standard in addition to building 333 new ones, which are identifiable by their square headlight recesses. About the same time, the vehicle was renamed AAVP7A1.

Weight:	56,552 pounds
Size (LxWxH):	321.3" x 128.7" x 130.5"
Max Speed, land:	30 mph
Max Speed, water:	6 mph
Range, land:	300 miles
Currently in use.	

Crooked Creek Publishing

Condition code	6	5	4	3	2	1	Rarity
Value (dollars)	1,000	3,500	6,000	8,000	11,000	13,500	2

M29 Weasel

The performance of the M28 proved to the Army that it had a winner on its hands. The M29 just fined-tuned the design. Essentially the same Studebaker Champion engine was used, but now the conventional automotive layout was used. The engine was mounted in front, with the transmission attached to it. A driveshaft transmitted the power to the rear steering differential.

Seating was increased from two to four, the tracks were of an improved design and the number of road wheels was doubled. The suspension system was vastly improved as well, largely solving the track-throwing problems previously experienced.

The tracks were further improved mid-production when their width was increased from 15" wide to 20". Studebaker built 4,476 of the M29 before switching production to the amphibious M29C.

The M29C had floatation cells added to each end of the vehicle, track aprons were installed, and dual rudders were mounted on the rear. The Weasel was propelled in the water by its tracks, which gave it a top speed of 4 mph in calm water. The M29C was the most abundant of the Weasels, with 10,647 being produced. Many of these had their flotation tanks and rudders removed in the field, essentially making them M29s.

Because the Weasel's remarkable performance in swamps, snow and water, it remained in the Army's inventory into the 1960s.

◆

M29
Weight: 3,725 pounds
Size (LxWxH): 126" x61" x71"
Max Speed: 36 mph
Range: 175 miles

◆

US Army TACOM LCMC

Condition code	6	5	4	3	2	1	Rarity
Value (dollars)	3,500	8,500	14,000	18,000	22,000	28,000	4

M116 Husky

By the late 1950s, the newest Weasel was nearing 15 years old and a program to create its replacement was undertaken. Pacific Car and Foundry Co. designed the Husky and built four pilot and three preproduction models by 1961. After testing, and a few recommended modifications, the vehicle was designated the M116 and a contract was issued for the vehicle to be placed in production. Surprisingly, the Blaw-Knox Co., famed for building huge radio antennas and construction equipment, won the bid to build the 197 production units. Pacific wasn't out of the fight yet, and it won contracts to build 111 of the M116A1 for the Navy and Marine Corps.

The Chevrolet V8 with Hydramatic transmission powerplant was positioned behind the driver. Its cooling air was drawn through a grille in the roof and exhausted through a grille on the right side of the vehicle.

A hinged door in the rear of the hull provided entrance and exit to the cargo space, and a winch was mounted on the front of the vehicle. The cargo area floor was moveable and could be raised to provide a flat cargo floor or lowered to provide troop seats. A canvas cargo cover and bows could cover the cargo space or a hard winter top could be mounted.

The Husky had a welded aluminum hull and fiberglass cab for light weight. The Husky had a load rating of 1 1/2 tons on both land and water. Water propulsion was by its spinning tracks.

Weight:	10,600 pounds
Size (LxWxH):	188" x 82" x 79"
Max Speed, land:	37 mph
Max Speed, water:	4.2 mph
Range:	300 miles

US Army TACOM LCMC

Tracked Vehicles

Condition code	6	5	4	3	2	1	Rarity
Value (dollars)	4,500	10,000	15,000	20,000	23,000	28,000	3

M548 Carrier

Originally developed for the Signal Corps as a carrier for radar systems, the M548 went on to be used in a variety of roles. Among these were ammunition carrier for the M107, M108, M109 and M110 self-propelled artillery pieces, as well as a Lance missile carrier.

Although one can hardly tell from appearances, the M548 was built using automotive components of the M113A1 family of vehicles. Hence, as improvements were made in the M113A1, similar improvements were made to the M548. As the M113A1 was upgraded to M113A2, the same changes were applied to the M538, resulting in the M548A1. In addition, the M548A1 had a 1,500-pound capacity chain hoist added in the cargo compartment.

Later, as the 6V53T turbosupercharged engine and Allison X200-4 cross drive transmission were added to the M113, resulting in the M113A3, some of the M548A1s were similarly upgraded. These changes not only made driver training easier, but also made the Carrier's performance equal to that of the Army's front-line fighting equipment

◆

M548A1
Weight: 28,300 pounds
Size (LxWxH): 232" x 105.75" x 110.75"
Max Speed, land: 35 mph
Range: 300 miles

◆

Self-Propelled Artillery

Allied-Axis

Condition code	6	5	4	3	2	1	Rarity
Value (dollars)	7,000	12,000	20,000	30,000	40,000	50,000	4

M7 Priest

This vehicle got its name from the pulpit-like appearance of the anti-aircraft machine gun ring and mount. Hardly a mobile sanctuary though, the M7 Priest family of vehicles was designed to provide armored units with highly mobile organic artillery support.

Between April 1942 and August 1943, American Locomotive Co. built 2,814 of these self-propelled guns based on components of the M3 medium tank chassis.

Experience in battle showed room for improvement and the next batch, built in mid-1944 by American Locomotive (500) and Federal Machine and Welder Co. (176) were somewhat modified. The most readily visible difference between the early and late models was the addition of fold down armor along the sides and rear of the fighting compartment.

Concurrently, Pressed Steel Car Co. was building 826 M7B1 self-propelled guns. The M7B1 was very similar to the late M7s, but was based on M4A3 components. Like the late M7, the M7B1's lower hulls were built of mild steel plate, not armor.

To increase the elevation of the howitzer for better use in the rugged terrain of Korea, during the 1950s many vehicles were converted to the M7B2 configuration. This was done by raising the gun mount and heightening the "pulpit," creating a very different looking vehicle.

◆

Weight: 52,000 pounds
Size (LxWxH): 237" x 117" x 104"
Max Speed: 24 mph
Armament: one 105mm howitzer, one .50-caliber machine gun

◆

Condition code	6	5	4	3	2	1	Rarity
Value (dollars)	7,000	15,000	25,000	35,000	45,000	58,000	4

M10 Gun Motor Carriage

U.S. Army doctrine prior to and during World War II was that enemy tanks were not to be fought with tanks; rather they were to be countered with tank destroyers. Various specialized vehicles were built for this purpose. Some, like the M6, were wheeled; others were built on half-track chassis. But the successful ones were fully track-laying vehicles that themselves very much resembled tanks. The M10 Tank Destroyer was such a vehicle, and was based on the automotive components of the diesel-powered M4A2 Sherman tank. Fisher Tank Arsenal built 4,993 of these vehicles, named Wolverines, between September 1942 and December 1943. The three-inch gun M7 was installed as its primary weapon.

A similar vehicle, based on the gasoline-powered M4A3, was built by Ford from October 1942 until September 1943. These 1,038 vehicles were known as the M10A1. Fisher also built 375 M10A1 vehicles.

Three different versions of turrets were mounted on the M10 series vehicles. Originally, the turret had no counterweights on the rear but, due to the imbalance caused by the gun, it was difficult to rotate the turret when the vehicle was on a slope.

Field units improvised various types of counterweights in an attempt to overcome this deficiency. Eventually, new vehicles were factory equipped with two 1,800-pound counterweights attached to the turret rear to correct this. Even later, the rear of the turret was redesigned and new counterweights were designed that included a small amount of storage space in them.

Unlike typical Army policy at the time, the diesel-powered M10s were deployed overseas, while the gas-powered versions were retained in the U.S. for training use.

Later, many of these retained M10s were rebuilt into M36 Gun Motor Carriages. Even later, some of the M10s were rebuilt with 90mm guns, becoming M36B2 Gun Motor Carriages. The British rearmed some of their M10s with a 17-pound Mk V, yielding a very effective tank killer dubbed the Achilles IIC.

Weight:	65,200 pounds
Size (LxWxH):	286.3" x 120" x 114"
Max Speed:	26 mph
Armament:	One three-inch gun, one .50-caliber machine gun

Simon Thomson

Condition code	6	5	4	3	2	1	Rarity
Value (dollars)	7,000	15,000	25,000	35,000	45,000	60,000	4

M36 Tank Destroyer

With the Allied forces facing such formidable foes as the German Tigers and Jagdpanthers, the three-inch gun was no longer adequate armament for a tank destroyer. Therefore, a 90mm weapon was trial fitted to a M10 tank destroyer. The weapon selected for this installation was a modification of the M1 90mm Anti-Aircraft gun, known as the T7 90mm gun. The results were sufficiently encouraging to warrant further testing. While the weapon and chassis were both adequate, the M10 turret was not suitable for the new weapon.

In March 1943, a development project was initiated and a contract written whereby Chevrolet would construct a wooden mockup and two soft steel pilot vehicles of the new 90mm Gun Motor Carriage T71. After Chevrolet built the wooden mockup, the decision was reached to transfer the production of the two pilot models to the Ford Motor Co., which completed them in September 1943. After a number of detail modifications, the T71 was ready for production.

These vehicles were to be constructed by remanufacturing 500 M10A1 three-inch gun motor carriages. In November 1943, the Fisher Tank Division of General Motors was requested to do this work, as the prime contractor for the M10A1. However, 200 of the vehicles were too near completion to be readily converted to the new configuration. To overcome this deficit, the remaining 200 vehicles were converted from vehicles returned from the field or depot stocks. To prevent this remanufacturing from slowing work at Fisher, this work was transferred to the Massey-Harris Co., Racine, Wis. Fisher built all the turrets for the T71s, both for its use as well as Massey-Harris.

In June 1944, the T71 was standardized as the M36. As the demand for M36 continued to rise, contracts were let with American Locomotive Co. to convert additional M10A1s into 90mm Gun Motor Carriages.

◆

Weight:	61,000 pounds
Size (LxWxH):	294" x 120" x 126"
Max Speed:	26 mph
Armament:	one 90mm cannon, one .50-caliber machine gun

◆

Self-Propelled Artillery | 343

Simon Thomson

Condition code	6	5	4	3	2	1	Rarity
Value (dollars)	7,000	15,000	25,000	35,000	45,000	60,000	4

M18 Hellcat Gun Motor Carriage

The M18 was as close to the ideal as was ever achieved for a tank destroyer under World War II U.S. Army doctrine. It was armed with the deadly 76mm gun, capable of defeating most enemy vehicles, and its top speed of 50 allowed it to get in and out of action quickly.

Production of the M18 Hellcat began in June 1943. At that time, the vehicle was known as the T70. It was reclassified at the M18 in March 1944. Buick continued to turn out the vehicles until October 1944, and 2,507 were produced.

The open-topped turret was constructed of welded armor and mounted a 76mm gun. The hull was also made of welded armor, and housed a driver and assistant driver, both of which had controls with which to drive the vehicle.

The armor of the M18 was very light and could be penetrated by a .30-caliber machine gun at 75 yards. The M18's greatest defense was its high speed.

The torsion bar suspension of the M18 provided a smooth ride, even at its high speeds.

Weight:	39,000 pounds
Size (LxWxH):	262" x 113" x 101"
Max Speed:	50 mph
Armament:	One 76mm cannon, one .50-caliber machine gun

Verne Kindischi

Not available on the collector market

M40/M43

The M40 was a 155mm gun motor carriage intended to replace the earlier M12. These vehicles saw extremely limited use in World War II, with only two trial vehicles being sent to Europe. But, like the Pershing and other late-war weapons, they saw extensive use in the Korean War. Though the Army had been slow to warm up to the idea of self-propelled artillery (the earlier M12 155mm Gun Motor Carriage was produced in small numbers and languished in storage for more than a year), by mid-war the Army wanted a new self-propelled large-caliber field piece.

Because the newly developed 155mm gun M1 was too heavy for installation on the same carriage the M12 used, a new design was begun. Ultimately it was decided that the new gun motor carriage would incorporate many of the components of the M4A3E8 into a newly designed chassis.

Production began by Pressed Steel Car Co. in February 1945, even before the

vehicle had been standardized as 155mm Gun Motor Carriage, M40. Production of the M40 totaled 418 pieces.

The M43, shown here, was an eight-inch howitzer mounted on the same chassis. Originally referred to as T89 Howitzer Motor Carriages, in November 1943 they were standardized as M43.

Designed to be readily convertible to 155mm Gun Motor Carriages, reversible travel locks and ammo racks able to handle either shell were installed. Pressed Steel's original order was for 576 pieces, but when the war ended only 24 had been produced and a further 24 were converted from M40 155mm Gun Motor Carriages.

◆

M43
Weight: 80,000 pounds
Size (LxWxH): 289" x 124" x 130"
Max Speed: 24 mph
Range: 107 miles

◆

US Army TACOM LCMC

Condition code	6	5	4	3	2	1	Rarity
Value (dollars)	6,500	9,000	14,000	20,000	26,000	35,000	3

M42 Duster

As tank chassis evolved, so did support vehicles built on tank chassis. The M42 was the successor to the M19 and, like the M19, was armed with dual automatic Bofors 40mm anti-aircraft cannon. The earliest production vehicles had conical shaped naval-style flash suppressors on the gun muzzles, but later production vehicles used a three-prong type. A .30-caliber machine gun was pintle mounted on the side of the turret for close-in defense.

A six-man crew served the Duster: the driver and commander riding in the hull, and a four-man gun crew including two loaders to feed the voracious appetite of the weapon, a sight setter and a gunner. These four men rode in the open-topped turret.

When fuel injection was added to the AOS-895-5 engine, the vehicles affected were classified as M42A1.

With the speed of aircraft increasing, the usefulness of the Duster as an anti-aircraft weapon became questionable. However, during the Vietnam conflict, the Duster with its twin Bofors cannon was employed very effectively against enemy troop formations. Even in dense jungle, the heavy 40mm shell was devastating, as it also was in urban settings.

◆

M42A1
Weight: 49,500 pounds
Size (LxWxH): 250" x 127" x 112"
Max Speed: 45 mph
Range: 100 miles

◆

Condition code	6	5	4	3	2	1	Rarity
Value (dollars)	7,000	15,000	25,000	35,000	45,000	60,000	5

M55 Eight-Inch Self-propelled Howitzer and M53 155mm Self-propelled Gun

Styled similarly to the smaller M52 105mm Self-propelled Howitzer, the M55 shown here was one of the largest vehicles fielded by the U.S. in Vietnam.

Though its engine and transmission were located in the front of the vehicle, the M55 was nonetheless based on the automotive components of the M48 tank. Pacific Car and Foundry, the vehicle's builder, used both the AV-1790-7B engine and CD-850-4B transmission to simplify logistics that powered these vehicles. The large turret at the rear of the M53 housed a 155mm cannon, while the M55 mounted an eight-inch howitzer.

Since they used the same chassis, many M53s were converted to M55s during the Vietnam War.

◆

Weight:	98,000 pounds
Size (LxWxH):	311" x 133" x 137"
Max Speed:	30 mph
Armament:	One eight-inch howitzer

◆

M44 Self-propelled Howitzer

This vehicle was designed to use as many of the automotive components of the M41 light tank as possible. It was hoped that this would reduce costs and simplify logistics. As originally built, the fighting compartment was enclosed. During testing, it was found that fumes from firing the 155mm howitzer were hampering the crew, and Massey-Harris stopped production after only 250 units were built. The vehicle was almost totally redesigned. Among changes were the opening of the top of the fighting compartment and the replacement of the main T97E1 howitzer with the T186E1 howitzer.

New production began and the 250 initial vehicles were rebuilt into the new configuration as well. The vehicles were finally accepted by the Army in 1952. When the engine was changed to the fuel injected AOSI-895-5, the designation changed to M44A1.

The M44A1 was used through the early 1970s.

Weight: 64,000 pounds
Size (LxWxH): 242.5" x 127.5" x 122.5"
Max Speed: 35 mph
Armament: One 155mm howitzer

LaPorte County Historical Society

Too few complete Ontos exist in private hands to establish value.

M50 Ontos

Ontos is Greek for "Thing" and, given the unusual appearance of this vehicle with its six recoilless rifles and oddly shaped hull, the name certainly fits.

The Ontos was conceived as a potent airborne tank destroyer. In November 1950, work began designing this beast. The requirements laid down by the Ordnance office were basic: The engine would be the inline six-cylinder GMC 302 used in the then-new G-749 family of 2 1/2-ton M135/M211 trucks. It was to be coupled to an Allison cross drive transmission, and its weight and dimension were to permit it to be carried inside the cargo aircraft of the day.

Of the 1,000 units in the original procurement plan, only 297 were produced beginning in 1955. Production ceased in November 1957, and the entire series was rejected by the Army. The Marine Corps was interested and took delivery of the vehicles, 176 of which were repowered with a Chrysler 361 cubic-inch

V-8 (some sources say 294) beginning in 1963, which required redesigned armored engine covers. The new cover extended forward of the rifle's travel lock, and engine access door gained louvers. With the new powerplant, the vehicle was redesignated M50A1.

While the six M40A1C 106mm recoilless rifles gave the Ontos tremendous firepower, its shortcoming was the requirement that the vehicle be opened up and a crewman expose himself in order to reload. They began to be phased out of service in the late 1960s.

Weight:	19,050 pounds
Size (LxWxH):	294" x 150.75" x 84"
Max Speed:	30 mph
Armament:	Six 106mm recoilless rifle, four .50-caliber spotting rifle, one .30-caliber machine gun

M56 Scorpion

One of the most unusual looking vehicles fielded by the Army was the M56 Scorpion. Cadillac began building the M56 in 1957 at its Cleveland tank plant. Ultimately, 325 of the self-propelled anti-tank guns rolled off the line. Armed with a 90mm gun and manned by a crew of four, the Scorpion was intended to be an airmobile anti-tank weapon.

The lightweight and basic design of the M56 omitted weather protection for the four-man crew. To the left of the manually elevated and traversed main gun was the driver's station and controls, with a windshield incorporated in the gun splinter shield. To the driver's left was the radio equipment, which formed the base of the commander's seat. The other two crew members rode on the other side of the breech.

The hull of the vehicle was of aluminum construction, with the splinter shield the only real armor on the vehicle.

A Continental six-cylinder horizontally-opposed gasoline engine powered the Scorpion. Its running gear was unusual in that it featured pneumatic tires on the four road wheels on each side. The Scorpion was used by the 82nd and 101st Airborne Divisions only from 1957 until 1970, including service in Vietnam.

The big gun, however, was deemed too powerful for the light chassis. When fired, the recoil would lift the front of the vehicle off the ground.

◆

Weight: 15,500 pounds
Size (LxWxH): 230" x 101.5" x 81"
Max Speed: 28 mph
Armament: 90mm gun M54

◆

US Army TACOM LCMC

M107 175mm Self-propelled Gun

Pacific Car and Foundry began delivering the M107 in 1962. These vehicles, and others on the same chassis, played a prominent role in Vietnam. Though self-propelled, the chassis with the big gun could scarcely be considered mobile. Its 13-man crew would establish a fire base, emplace the weapon and thus command the battlefield for a 20-mile radius.

The gun was on a rotating mount at the rear of the open vehicle. The mount could be rotated 30 degrees either side of center, and the gun elevated to 65 degrees.

A spade at the rear of the hull anchored the vehicle during firing. In later years, both FMC and Bowen-McLaughlin-York produced the M107.

Regardless of who built it, the M107 with its incredibly long gun tube was unmistakable.

◆

Weight:	62,100 pounds
Size (LxWxH):	444.8" x 124" x 136.8"
Max Speed:	34 mph
Armament:	175mm gun M113

◆

Tracked Vehicles

US Army TACOM LCMC

M110 Eight-inch Howitzer

The M110 eight-inch howitzer was produced concurrently with the M107, with which it shared a chassis. Like the M107, the M110 also was built originally by Pacific Car and Foundry, and later by FMC and BMY.

Torsion bar suspension equipped with five dual rubber-tired roadwheels on each side supported the vehicle. The drive sprocket was at the front and the fifth roadwheel acted as the idler. The return run of track ran out the top of the roadwheels. The vehicles were powered by a Detroit Diesel Model 8V-71T diesel engine, driving through an Allison Transmission XTG-411-2A cross-drive transmission at the front of the hull.

The M110 was also used extensively in Vietnam. Though its range was only about half that of the M107, its 200-pound round had a reputation for greater accuracy and ease of use than the 175mm round.

Weight: 58,500 pounds
Size (LxWxH): 294.4" x 124" x 115.6"
Max Speed: 34 mph
Armament: Eight-inch howitzer M2A2

M110A2 Eight-inch Howitzer

The M110A1 began replacing the M110 in 1976. Its main weapon was a M201 eight-inch howitzer. This had a much longer barrel than the M2A2 and longer range.

However, the quest for range was not over. A double-baffle muzzle brake was added to the tube, making it a M201A1. The reduction of recoil forces provided by the muzzle brake allowed the weapon to fire the M188A1 propelling charge at zone nine, rather than zone eight. This translates to a range of 16,800 meters. If that was not sufficient, a rocket-assisted projectile could be used, with a range of 30,000 meters.

The complete self-propelled howitzers, so modified, were known as M110A2, and all the U.S. Army and Marine Corps M107s were rearmed.

These vehicles were withdrawn from service in the 1990s.

◆

Weight: 62,500 pounds
Size (LxWxH): 422.5" x 124" x 123"
Armament: Eight-inch howitzer M201A1

◆

Tracked Vehicles

US Army TACOM LCMC

M109A1 Self-propelled Howitzer

The big gun, fully enclosed turret and tracks lead many casual observers to believe this vehicle is a tank. However, it is self-propelled artillery and its armor is of little use against anything more substantial than an infantryman's rifle.

Development of this family of vehicles began in the late 1950s. Early on there was a M108 variant that was armed with a 105mm howitzer, but it was soon discontinued in favor of its companion vehicle, the 155mm howitzer armed M109. Production of both vehicles began in 1962. Production of the M108 ended in 1963, while production of the M109 continued until 1969. All the M109s were built in the Cleveland tank plant, but depending upon the contract and year of manufacture the builders were Cadillac Motor Car division of General Motors, Chrysler Corp. and Allison Division of General Motors.

The Army bought 1,961 M109s, while the Marines bought 150 more. Though not as often photographed in the country as were the open-topped M107 and M110, the M109s were deployed to Vietnam. It was there that it was learned that the T255E4 155mm weapon mounted in the vehicle, when firing the XM1119 propelling charge for maximum range, caused serious damage to both the vehicle and its crew.

Installing the longer barreled M185 howitzer solved this problem. Very little modification to the vehicle was necessary to accomplish this, with the result being the M109A1. In 1972, mass conversion began of the M109 fleet into the M109A1 configuration. Bowen-McLaughlin-York began producing factory-fresh M109A1s from scratch in 1974.

Weight:	53,060 pounds
Size (LxWxH):	356.3" x 124" x 129.1"
Max Speed:	35 mph
Armament:	155mm howitzer M185, one .50 M2 HB Machine Gun

US Army TACOM LCMC

M109A2 Self-propelled Howitzer

Troops in the field suggested various changes to the weapon system based on their first-hand experiences, many of which were incorporated into the M109A2. Chief among these was the request for more ammo storage. Accordingly, the turret bustle was enlarged to add storage for eight more rounds. A new gun mount was installed and the flotation equipment removed as well. From 1976 through 1985, 823 of these new vehicles were supplied to the Army. Many of the earlier M109A1 vehicles were also updated to this new standard and these rebuilt vehicles were classified M109A3.

In the mid-1980s, the M109 family was upgraded to include nuclear, chemical biological (NBC) protection for the crew. As the M109A2 and M109A3 vehicles received these upgrades, they were reclassified as M109A4.

◆

Weight:	53,060 pounds
Size (LxWxH):	356.3" x 124" x 129.1"
Max Speed:	35 mph
Armament:	155mm howitzer M185, one .50 M2 HB Machine Gun

◆

US Army TACOM LCMC

M109A6 Paladin

The name of the latest variant of the M109 family has special meaning to fans of late 1950s-early 1960s TV westerns. First delivered in April 1992, the M109A6 Paladin introduced improved armor, armament, increased ammunition stowage and NBC equipment, including micro-climate cooling for the crewmen. The biggest change was the automatic fire control system including automatic gun laying and power-assisted semiautomatic loading. The Paladin can go from road march to pinpoint firing in less than 60 seconds.

Due to the relatively high cost of the Paladin, reserve units were supplied with a more economical alternative, the M109A5. The M109A5 was created by upgrading older vehicles with the new M284 howitzer and M182 mount as used on the Paladin. A NBC protection system comparable to that of the M109A4 was also installed. Both the M109A5 and M109A6 weapons have a maximum range of 30 kilometers.

◆

Weight:	56,400 pounds
Size (LxWxH):	386" x 154.4" x 127.4"
Max Speed:	38 mph
Armament:	155mm howitzer M284, one .50-caliber M2 HB Machine Gun

◆

Half Track Vehicles

Pat Stansell

Condition code	6	5	4	3	2	1	Scarcity
Value (dollars)	1,500	4,000	9,500	15,000	22,000	29,000	4

M2 Half Track

An Ordnance Committee meeting authorized the conversion of a M2A1 Scout Car into a half track for test purposes (this should at last put to rest the question of "is a scout car a wheeled half track, or is a half track a track-laying scout car?"). Though underpowered, overall this vehicle was satisfactory. At the conclusion of the tests, the vehicle was converted back into standard M2A1 Scout Car configuration.

An outgrowth of this test was the T14 authorized in 1939. Developed by White Motor Co., this vehicle was intended to serve as an artillery prime mover and very much resembled the later M2. The specifications for the M2 were laid down after the T14 tests, and invitations for bids circulated. The Autocar Co. of Ardmore, Pa., was the lowest bidder and was awarded a contract for the production of 424 M2 Half Track Cars.

By fall of 1940, the demand for M2 and M3 half tracks had exceeded the production capacity of any one firm. The three lowest of the original bidders: Autocar, Diamond T and White, were all contracted to produce vehicles. In a precursor to the later M-series standardization, it was decided that the half tracks produced by all three firms be alike and that parts should be totally interchangeable. The Half Track Engineering Committee, consisting of representative of all three firms, as well as the Army, was formed to carry out this plan. Representatives of International Harvester were later invited to join this committee.

◆

M2A1
Weight: 15,100 pounds
Size (LxWxH): 242" x 87.5" x 89"
Max Speed: 45 mph
Range: 210 miles

◆

Pat Stansell

Condition code	6	5	4	3	2	1	Scarcity
Value (dollars)	1,500	4,000	9,500	15,000	22,000	29,000	3

Carrier, Personnel, Half Track M3

The M3 half track had a body slightly longer than that of the M2. The chassis itself was 10" longer. To fulfill the role of personnel carrier, the M3 had a door in the rear of the body and bench seats along the body sides. It was intended that this vehicle be provided to armored divisions and motorized infantry units.

Mechanically, the M3 was identical to the M2, sharing its powerplant, suspension and forward armor. The M3 used an M25 pedestal mount to support its M2HB anti-aircraft machine gun and the rear of the vehicle was reinforced to stabilize the gun when firing.

The Autocar Co. initially produced this vehicle. Diamond T and White later joined Autocar in production. White built fewer than 200 of the 12,499 M3 half tracks produced, making them very rare today.

Beware, many half tracks on the market today have reproduction armor installed on them, the original having been cut away long ago.

◆

Weight:	15,500 pounds
Size (LxWxH):	250" x 87.5" x 89"
Max Speed:	45 mph
Range:	210 miles

◆

Pat Stansell

Condition code	6	5	4	3	2	1	Scarcity
Value (dollars)	1,500	4,000	9,500	15,000	22,000	29,000	3

Carrier, Personnel, Half Track M3A1

Just as the skate rail of the M2 was replaced with a M49 ring mount, so was the pedestal mount of the M3. Beginning in October 1943, the reconfigured vehicle, standardized as the Carrier, Personnel, Half Track, M3A1, was placed in production. By the time all M3A1 half track production ceased in February 1944, 2,862 of these carriers had been built.

Few vehicles say "Vintage Military Vehicle" like the half track. No doubt this is in part due to the U.S. military completely abandoning production of this type vehicle even before the war ended, as well as civilian counterparts being few and far between. While the high cost of replacement track limits the drivability of these vehicles, they remain head-turners today.

Weight:	15,300 pounds
Size (LxWxH):	250" x 87.5" x 106"
Max Speed:	45 mph
Range:	210 miles

Tracked Vehicles

Condition code	6	5	4	3	2	1	Scarcity
Value (dollars)	2,500	6,000	14,000	20,000	29,000	38,000	4

Note: value with dummy weapons.

M16 Multiple Gun Motor Carriage

Various anti-aircraft mounts using a variety of weapons were tried using the half track chassis as a basis. The most successful of these was the M16 Multiple Gun Motor Carriage. The Maxson was mounted 6" from the floor so the machine guns could be fired horizontally over the folding side flaps of the half track.

The firepower of the quad .50-caliber mount, which had the combined ability to fire 2,200 rounds per minute, was lethal against any aircraft it could get into its sights. The M16 was also used in Korea where, in addition to aircraft, the massed firepower of the quad mount was used against ground targets, with devastating effects.

White built 2,877 M16s between May 1943 and March 1944. In addition to these, 568 M13 Multiple Gun Motor and 109 T10E1 twin 20mm Multiple Gun Motor Carriages were converted to M16 Multiple Gun Motor Carriages.

All factory-produced M16 Multiple Gun Motor Carriages were equipped with the front-mounted PTO-driven Tulsa winch.

◆

Weight:	18,640 pounds
Size (LxWxH):	256" x 87.5" x 88"
Max Speed:	45 mph
Range:	210 miles

◆

Tracked Vehicles

Simon Thomson

Condition code	6	5	4	3	2	1	Scarcity
Value (dollars)	1,500	4,000	9,500	15,000	22,000	29,000	3

M5 and M5A1 Half Tracks

The demand for half track vehicles exceeded not only the production capacity of White, Autocar and Diamond T, but the demand for component parts. Engines, axles, armor and transmissions also taxed the limits of the suppliers. In April 1942, an alternate supplier was sought that would alleviate all these bottlenecks. The International Harvester Co. was selected to produce a similar vehicle, but using different sources of supply for the critical components.

International used its own engine, the 450 Red Diamond, as well as producing its own transmission and axles for this project. Because of advancements made in welding armor plate between 1940 and 1942, it was decided that the bodies of the new vehicles would be built of welded homogenous 5/16" armor plate. Welded construction offered better protection by reducing the risk of bullet splash entering

the crew compartment and eliminating any danger of armored bolts shearing and becoming projectiles inside the vehicle. Other notable differences include the use of 9.00-20 front tires on the IH vehicles and rounded rear corners on the body. Half tracks by other makers had square corners.

International would assemble the vehicles at its Springfield, Ohio, plant, with components being made at other Harvester facilities. The IH equivalent of the M3 was designated M5.

◆

M5A1
Weight: 15,100 pounds
Size (LxWxH): 242" x 87.5" x 106"
Max Speed: 42 mph
Range: 125 miles

◆

Pat Stansell

Condition code	6	5	4	3	2	1	Scarcity
Value (dollars)	1,500	4,000	9,500	15,000	22,000	29,000	3

M9A1 Half Track

The M2's counterpart was the M9. Initially it was requested that International Harvester build personnel carriers, but even before production had begun on these, a request was made to also produce the prime movers.

To simplify logistics, the IH-built half tracks were supplied as International Aid vehicles to other governments and employed in the United States as training vehicles, while U.S. combat troops received vehicles built by the other firms.

The first production M5 personnel carrier was completed Nov. 9, 1942, and the first M9A1 March 17, 1943. No M9 production vehicles were built. The decision had been made to adopt the ring mount prior to production commencing

on the skate rail-equipped vehicle. The first IH-produced, ring mount equipped personnel carrier was completed March 17, 1943, with mass production beginning three weeks later.

Fifty-seven percent of International's personnel carriers were equipped with winches; the balance featured unditching rollers. The ratio was 50-50 on prime movers, and it is believed similar ratios were employed by the other manufacturers.

◆

Weight: 15,100 pounds
Size (LxWxH): 242" x 87.5" x 106"
Max Speed: 42 mph
Range: 125 miles

◆

High Speed Tractors

Condition code	6	5	4	3	2	1	Scarcity
Value (dollars)	1,200	3,000	6,000	9,000	12,000	15,000	3

M2 High Speed Tractor

The smallest high-speed tractor in the Army's inventory was the M2 seven-ton tractor developed by the Cleveland Tractor Co. (Cletrac). These vehicles were produced not only by Cleveland, but also by John Deere. The M2 was widely used by the Army Air Force and many of the 8,510 built were used at airfields. In addition to being useful as a "tug" around the airfield, it also had a large air compressor mounted on the rear, which was very useful for airing up not only the tires but also the landing gear of various aircraft. The drawbar was especially designed to transfer as much weight as possible from the towed object to the tractor to increase the tractive effort available.

The M2 was powered by the 404 cubic-inch Hercules WXLC3 six-cylinder gasoline engine.

◆

Weight:	14,700 pounds
Size (LxWxH):	163" x 69" x 64"
Max Speed:	22 mph
Range:	100 miles

◆

CCP

Condition code	6	5	4	3	2	1	Scarcity
Value (dollars)	1,000	2,500	3,800	5,500	9,500	14,000	3

M4 High Speed Tractor

This series of 18-ton High Speed Tractors was designed and built by Allis-Chalmers. Like other high-speed tractors, it was equipped to not only tow the artillery pieces, but also to transport the artillery crew and a basic supply of ammunition.

Depending upon the type of artillery piece they were intended to tow, the M4s were built in two configurations. Those equipped to carry 90mm or three-inch ammunition were said to be fitted for a Class A load, while the Class B load was 155mm, 240mm or eight-inch ammo. A built-in crane and hoist eased the handling of the ammunition. Mounted on the rear of the vehicle was a PTO-driven 30,000-pull winch that was used positioning and setting up the artillery pieces. Production of the M4 series began in March 1943 and continued through June 1945, with a total of 5,552 units being assembled. Field experience in mud and snow made it desirable for the tractor to be equipped with wider tracks. This was accomplished

by adding duck-bill extensions to the ends of each track shoe. Of course, this necessitated the moving of the suspension units out from the hull. Only 259 units in this configuration, classified M4A1, were built, all between June and August 1945.

Some of these vehicles were modified to carry more munitions, reducing the crew from 11 to eight. These modified vehicles were identified by adding a C suffix to their model numbers.

In 1954, Bowen-McLaughlin began a rebuilding program on the M4 tractors. These updated tractors were classified M4A2. The M4 series of vehicles soldiered on with the U.S. Army through the mid-1960s before finally being declared obsolete and put up for disposal.

Weight:	31,400 pounds
Size (LxWxH):	210" x 97" x 108"
Max Speed:	35 mph
Range:	100 miles
Max towed load:	38,700 pounds

Crooked Creek Publishing

Condition code	6	5	4	3	2	1	Scarcity
Value (dollars)	900	2,400	3,000	4,500	8,500	12,000	3

M5 High Speed Tractor

One of the great assets of the U.S military during World War II was the mobility of its artillery units. U.S. artillery was almost totally mechanized, ranging from Gun and Howitzer Motor Carriages (self-propelled artillery in today's nomenclature) to artillery towed with wheeled prime movers, which depending upon the piece could be anything from a Jeep to a huge Mack NO 7 1/2-ton prime mover. High-speed crawler tractors filled the niche between the extremes of using a truck to tow a weapon and making the artillery self-propelled.

The military's idea of "high speed" isn't the same as what civilians consider high speed. Rather it serves to distinguish these vehicles from the "normal" crawler tractors, similar to bulldozers, which had been used as artillery prime movers prior to this and continued to be used alongside the high speed tractors briefly.

The tractors were designed and built by International Harvester at its Bettendorf, Iowa, works.

The M5 was a 13-ton high-speed, full-track, prime mover, which was used for towing the 90mm AA gun, 4.5-inch gun, and 155mm howitzer.

They cost the government approximately $14,000 each.

Weight:	28,572 pounds
Size (LxWxH):	191.25" x 100" x 104"
Max Speed:	30 mph
Range:	150 miles
Max towed load:	20,000 pounds

Condition code	6	5	4	3	2	1	Scarcity
Value (dollars)	900	2,400	3,000	4,500	8,500	12,000	3

M5A1 High Speed Tractor

Introduced in May 1945, the M5A1 was essentially a M5 with a steel cab fitted in lieu of the soft canvas cab structure of the M5. Comparatively few of this type of vehicle were built, with production totaling only 589 when the assembly line closed in August 1945.

A horizontal volute suspension system was developed for these tractors. This suspension system was retrofitted to many of the vehicles after the war. When the vertical volute suspension of an M5 was replaced with the HVSS, the vehicle was redesignated M5A2. A similar change to a M5A1 resulted in a M5A3. The M5-series of tractors was phased out of service by the U.S. military in the early 1960s.

A rear-mounted Continental R6572 straight six-cylinder engine powered the M5 series vehicles.

A 15,000-pound capacity PTO-driven winch was provided at the front of the tractor. While it could be used for vehicle recovery, its primary purpose was for use when emplacing the artillery piece the vehicle towed.

Weight:	30,405 pounds
Size (LxWxH):	196.5" x 100" x 104"
Max Speed:	30 mph
Range:	150 miles
Max towed load:	20,000 pounds

Tracked Vehicles

US Army TACOM LCMC

Condition code	6	5	4	3	2	1	Scarcity
Value (dollars)	900	2,400	3,000	4,500	8,500	12,000	3

M39 Armored Utility Vehicle

Using 640 returned M18 Hellcat tank destroyers as a basis, in 1944 Buick began constructing the M39 armored utility vehicle. The M18 was an extraordinarily fast vehicle, with a top speed of 60 mph. Hence, the M39, with the same performance, was truly a "high speed tractor."

A need had been identified for a high-speed fully tracked vehicle that could be used alternately in an armored reconnaissance role, as a high-speed tractor or as an armored personnel carrier. In the latter capacity, the T41, as the M39 was originally known, was hampered by having space for only eight troops in the cargo area.

The U.S. Army used the M39 through 1957.

◆

Weight:	35,500 pounds
Size (LxWxH):	214" x 113" x 77.5"
Max Speed:	60 mph
Range:	155 miles
Max towed load:	10,000 pounds

◆

M6 High Speed Tractor

Built by Allis-Chalmers, the M6 was the king of the World War II high-speed tractors. Powered by two huge Waukesha 145GZ gasoline engines, giving it a towing capacity up to 60,000 pounds, the M6 could handle the toughest of the prime mover jobs. The two 817 cubic-inch engines drove the vehicle through torque converters and a constant mesh two-speed transmission. The big engines were quite thirsty, with the 250-gallon fuel tank only providing a range of 110 miles. Top speed with the weapon in tow was 20 miles per hour.

Two of the big A-Cs were needed to tow the massive field pieces: one towed the cannon tube, the other towed the carriage. Upon arrival at the field position, the several-hour assembly process of the artillery piece began, usually with the assistance of a crane. While moving the cannon, the M6 also transported the crews for the weapons and, depending upon the caliber, it also carried 20 to 24 rounds of ammunition.

The M6 was equipped with an impressive 60,000-pound capacity drag winch in the rear, which was used assembling and positioning the artillery.

The crew of 11 men sat in two rows in the front of the vehicle, the engines were in the middle with the radiators on either side and ammunition boxes were on the rear of the tractor. An M49C ring mount for the M2 Browning .50 caliber machine gun was mounted on the roof for defense.

Production of these huge machines didn't get under way in LaPorte until February 1944, and by August 1945 only 1,235 had been built.

Weight:	76,000 pounds
Size (LxWxH):	258" x 120.5" x 104"
Max Speed:	21 mph
Range:	100 miles
Max towed load:	50,000 pounds

Too few complete examples exist to establish pricing.

Armored Recovery Vehicles

Condition code	6	5	4	3	2	1	Scarcity
Value (dollars)	15,000	24,000	30,000	40,000	50,000	60,000	5

M32A1B3 Tank Recovery Vehicle

In an effort to provide a maximum amount of parts commonality between tank retrievers and the vehicles they were to support, four types of Sherman-based recovery vehicles were built. Based on the M4, M4A1, M4A2 and M4A3 chassis, respectively, were the M32, M32B1, M32B2 and M32B3. A M32B4 based upon the M4A4 was planned, but never reached production.

At the request of the Marine Corps, the M32A1B3 shown here was developed, based on the horizontal volute suspension system (HVSS) equipped M4A3E8. Baldwin Locomotive Works and International Harvester in combination built 80 of this variant in 1945. Additional vehicles were converted after the war. Installation of the HVSS to the M32B1 resulted in the new designation M32A1B1.

Unlike the M31 series, the M32 series had a fixed dummy turret mounted. Instead of the M31's boom, there was an A-frame fitted to the front of the hull.

This A-frame swung forward for heavy lifting, but remained to the rear for towing other vehicles, being supported by yet another A-frame welded to the hull rear. A 60,000-pound Gar Wood winch was mounted in the hull, which could be used in conjunction with the A-frame for lifting, or the line run through openings in the hull for direct pulls.

The M32 also increased armament over the M31, being armed not only with .30-caliber bow weapon, but also a .50-caliber machine gun on the turret, and an 81mm mortar on the hull front. The intended use of the mortar was to lay down smoke barrages to mask recovery operations and it was ultimately eliminated.

Production of the M32-series began at Lima Locomotive works in June 1943.

◆

M32B3
Weight: 64,100 pounds
Size (LxWxH): 232" x 103" x 116"
Max Speed: 26 mph
Range: 130 miles

◆

Verne Kindischi

Condition code	6	5	4	3	2	1	Scarcity
Value (dollars)	15,000	24,000	30,000	40,000	50,000	60,000	4

M74 Tank Recovery Vehicle

The M26 Pershing tank, which went into combat in the closing phases of World War II, and the later M46 and M47 stretched the abilities of the M32 recovery vehicles to their limits. Accordingly, work was begun on a more substantial, better-equipped vehicle. The hundreds of M4A3 tanks in stock, and growing obsolete, made them ready candidates for such a tank retriever. Bowen McLauglin-York (BMY) developed such a vehicle, known as the M74, and began mass converting these units in February 1954. BMY finished its last conversion in October 1955. As the M74 was issued, the previously used M32B1 retrievers were turned in as surplus. Rock Island Arsenal then converted these into additional M74 retrievers, a process that lasted until 1958.

The M74 was a considerable improvement over the older model, not the least of which was an increase of winch capacity from the M32's 60,000 pounds to 90,000 pounds as well as the introduction of separate tow and lift winches. Also, the A frame of the M74 was now hydraulic elevated, and the vehicle was fitted with a front-mounted blade that could be used to anchor the retriever during heavy recovery operations or be used as a light bulldozer.

The M74 had a bow .30-caliber machine gun and a .50-caliber mounted on the commander's cupola.

◆

Weight: 93,750 pounds
Size (LxWxH): 313" x 121" x 133.5"
Max Speed: 21 mph
Range: 100 miles

◆

Patton Museum, Ft. Knox, Ky.

M51

This huge tank retriever was created using the suspension and automotive components of the M103 heavy tank. Just as the M103 was shunned by the Army but used by the Marines, so it was with the M51. The U.S. Marine Corps adopted the M51 in 1958 and used it through the Vietnam War and beyond. The Army preferred the M88.

Four men operated the M51, which was equipped with a hydraulically driven 45-ton capacity recovery winch as well as a five-ton auxiliary winch. A large, hydraulically actuated boom was mounted toward the rear of the vehicle. Anchor blades, also raised and lowered hydraulically, were provided both on the front and rear to stabilize the M51 during recovery and lifting operations.

The size of the M51 is put into scale by this photo of a B Company 2nd Tank Battalion 2nd Marine Division retriever backed up to a captured *Swedish Stridsvagn L60* in the Dominican Republic in May 1965.

◆

Weight:	120,000 pounds
Size (LxWxH):	399" x 143" x 129"
Max Speed:	30 mph
Range:	200 miles

◆

Not readily available.

US Army TACOM LCMC

Not readily available.

M88 Tank Recovery Vehicle

As the size and weight of America's tanks increased, it became evident that even the improved M74 would not be up to the task. In 1959, production of the M88 began by Bowen-McLaughlin-York Inc., of York, Pa., which had also designed the vehicle. The initial order was for 1,075 vehicles. Their design has proven to be very well thought out and durable.

The M88 is built on an armored chassis similar to a tank, and shares many components with the M48/M60 Medium Tank families. The lower portion of the hull is filled with two hydraulically powered winches, a hoist winch and a separate main winch. The 50,000-pound capacity hoist winch uses an A-frame boom and its 400 feet of 5/8-inch wire rope for heavy lifting. The main recovery winch is of 90,000-pound capacity and its drum holds 200 feet of 1.25-inch wire rope.

Any addition to the two winches, other hydraulically operated equipment includes a bow-mounted blade, boom, refueling pump and a very powerful impact wrench. The front-mounted bulldozer blade is used to hold and stabilize the retriever during heavy lifting and for all winching operations.

◆

Weight:	112,000 pounds
Size (LxWxH):	325.5" x 135" x 115"
Max Speed:	30 mph
Range:	222 miles

◆

US Army TACOM LCMC

M88A1 Tank Recovery Vehicle

The original M88 was powered by a gasoline engine. However, the Army decided to move to an all-diesel fleet of armored vehicles. Accordingly, the diesel-powered M88A1 was introduced. Additionally, a program to upgrade older M88s to A1 status was undertaken, which was finally completed in 1982.

The M88A1 engine is a 750-horsepower, turbosupercharged Continental M12, four-cycle, air-cooled, model AVDS-1790-2DR diesel. It drives the vehicle through an Allison XT-1410-4 cross drive transmission, which provides three forward and one reverse speed. The transmission is a combination transmission, differential, steering and braking unit.

The engine and final drive are located at the rear of the hull, the hoist winch in the middle, and the main winch is located between the hoist winch and the front of the retriever, under and between the driver's and mechanic's seats. Like the M88, the M88A1's crew of four includes a driver/operator, a mechanic, a rigger and a commander.

US Army TACOM LCMC

Not readily available.

M88A2 Tank Recovery Vehicle

In 1989, with 3,042 produced, M88A1 production ended, but the tooling was placed in storage. For years, the M88 had been the heaviest armored vehicle in the Army inventory, but that was changing. When the M1 Abrams debuted, the mighty M88A1, which could handle a M60 with ease, found itself struggling. Oftentimes two M88A1s were required to recover a single Abrams. This was the same situation that brought about the need three decades previously for the M74 to be replaced by the M88.

However, M88 and its designers, now a unit of United Defense, were not going to give up without a fight.

Upgrades to the M88A1 to improve its suspension and towing, winching, lifting and braking characteristics yielded the M88A2. Dubbed the Hercules, the M88A2 can singularly handle any tracked vehicle in the U.S. Army inventory. That this vehicle continues to serve is evidence of the soundness of the original, now 45 year-old, design.

Weight:	140,000 pounds
Size (LxWxH):	338" x 123" x 144"
Max Speed:	25 mph
Range:	200 miles

Condition code	6	5	4	3	2	1	Scarcity
Value (dollars)	5,000	10,000	15,000	24,000	30,000	40,000	5

M578 Recovery Vehicle

Among the smallest tracked recovery vehicles fielded by the U.S. Army is the M578. Chief among the reasons for its bantam weight is the fact that it was not originally designed to be a recovery vehicle at all! Rather, it was to be an air-transportable crane for replacing barrels on M107/M110 self-propelled guns, with which it shares a chassis. Ultimately, this T120 crane was equipped with a modicum of recovery gear and designated the M578 Light Armored Full Tracked Recovery Vehicle.

The front of the M578 is essentially the same as the chassis of the self-propelled guns. The engine is mounted to the right and the driver sits on the left, separated by an insulated metal firewall. Directly behind the power plant is an auxiliary drive, which powers the generator and the hydraulic pumps when the engine main engine is shut off. The M578 has two winches, a 30,000-pound boom winch and a 60,000-pound capacity drag winch.

The hydraulic pumps provide power for the winches, boom, cab and rear spade.

The crane cab houses the crew during recovery operations. Directly behind the crane operator's seat is a full height tool locker for recovery gear storage, accessible from outside the crane cab. While both the hull and crane cab are made of welded steel armor, it is intended to protect the crew only from small caliber bullets and shell splinters. The M578 is equipped with a M2 .50-caliber Browning machine gun for self-defense.

The powerplant for the M578 is the Detroit Diesel GMC 8V71T turbosupercharged eight-cylinder, V-type two-cycle diesel driving through an Allison model XTG-411-2A cross drive transmission.

◆

Weight:	54,000 pounds
Size (LxWxH):	250.25" x 124" x 130.5"
Max Speed:	37 mph
Range:	450 miles

◆

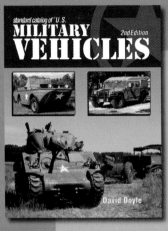